Strength
for the
Journey

Phil 4:13

Strength

for the

Journey

A Woman's Journey through Hospice

Kay Lukkarila

All glory goes to the Lord who gave me strength to do whatever I needed to do when it had to be done. He gave me strength for the moment and strength for the journey.

© 2018 Kay Lukkarila. All rights reserved.

Interior photos by Kay Lukkarila

Cover photo by Kay Lukkarila © 2017

"Soft and Tender Goodbye" music and lyrics ©2008 Todd Wuollet. Used by permission.

All hymns, songs and lyrics are public domain unless otherwise noted.

No part of this book may be reproduced, stored in a retrieval system, or transmitted by any means without the written permission of the author.

All Scripture quotations, unless otherwise indicated, are taken from THE HOLY BIBLE, NEW INTERNATIONAL VERSION®, NIV® Copyright © 1973, 1978, 1984, 2011 by Biblica, Inc.® Used by permission. All rights reserved worldwide.

Scripture quotations marked (NASB) are taken from the NEW AMERICAN STANDARD BIBLE®, Copyright © 1960, 1962, 1963, 1968, 1971, 1972, 1973, 1975, 1977, 1995 by The Lockman Foundation. Used by permission.

Scripture quotations marked (NLT) are taken from the Holy Bible, New Living Translation, copyright © 1996, 2004, 2007, 2013, 2015 by Tyndale House Foundation. Used by permission of Tyndale House Publishers, Inc., Carol Stream, Illinois 60188. All rights reserved.

Scripture quotations marked (NKJV) are taken from the New King James Version®. Copyright © 1982 by Thomas Nelson. Used by permission. All rights reserved.

Scriptures marked KJV are taken from the KING JAMES VERSION (KJV): KING JAMES VERSION, public domain

Because of the dynamic nature of the internet, any web addresses or links contained in this book may have changed since publication and may no longer be valid.

ISBN-13:978-1986758277
ISBN-10:1986758273

DEDICATION

Strength for the Journey is dedicated to my Lord and Savior Jesus Christ, who strengthened me during the difficult journey of cancer and hospice, and to my beloved Mom, Loraine Wuollet (1928-2008). May your love and kindness be remembered in the generations to come.

Contents

Acknowledgements...	ix
Prologue...	1
January: Planning the Party...............................	4
February 28: Mom's Birthday..............................	5
The Journey Begins...	7

March

The 2nd: March Madness...............................	8
The 7th: The Flu?...	9
The 10th: Doctor's Orders..............................	13
The 13th: The Diagnosis................................	17
Unexpected Journey......................................	21
The 15th: The Retreat...................................	22
The 21st: Hospice at Home.............................	25
The 24th: Aunts Swap Duties..........................	33
The 25th: Nothing Wrong with My Mind!............	37
The 26th: Rest..	43
The 27th: Moving Day...................................	45
The 28th: Conserving Energy..........................	51
The 29th: The Toothbrush..............................	56
The 30th: Don't Lose Heart............................	59
The 31st: Caregiver Plus...............................	61

April

The 1st: A Cheerful Heart..............................	63
The 3rd: The Best Driver...............................	65
The 4th: Air Hunger......................................	71
The 5th: Memories.......................................	75
The 8th: His Ways..	83
The 9th: Family...	85

The 11th: White as Snow.................................... 93
The 12th: Too Much Stuff.................................. 99
The 15th: Grandma Sitting Duties...................... 103
The 15th: Blessed Be Your Name....................... 105
The 17th: Lifeline.. 109
The 20th: Two Machines.................................. 113
The 22nd: Different Gifts................................. 117
The 25th: Weaker Voice................................... 123
The 27th: So Grateful...................................... 127
The 28th: Mottled Feet.................................... 129
The 30th: Someday Soon.................................. 131

May

The 1st: Imminent Signs................................... 135
The 2nd: The Annuity...................................... 140
The 3rd: God Awakens Mary.............................. 144
The 4th: Goodbyes Begin.................................. 149
The 5th: Soft and Tender Goodbye...................... 150
The 6th: Final Farewells.................................... 153
The 7th: The Last Day...................................... 155
The 28th: Strength for Every Step....................... 159
The 7th: One Year Later.................................... 163

Afterward.. 167
Notes... 170

Acknowledgements

Many thanks to Sarah Lukkarila, Kristin Salvevold, and Laverne Ronkainen for helping edit this book. Their wisdom, advice, and encouragement helped me continue writing and finishing the book. They sacrificed their time and talents to see this work completed. Thanks to Gretchyn Quernemoen who encouraged me and guided me through the process of self-publishing.

Words cannot even express how grateful I am to all who prayed for me as I wrote this book and all who encouraged me along the way. You held me accountable by asking me how the writing was coming along or how you could pray. The Lord used your faithfulness to complete this book.

I am extremely grateful to my husband, Chuck and our kids, Jim, Sarah, Rachel, and Jacob. They continued to encourage me through this whole process. When the book was more than an idea, they spurred me on to continue by asking how I was doing on the book and almost setting deadlines for me when I was overwhelmed. They helped me with the many computer problems I had and also gave me the time I needed to complete this endeavor. During Mom's illness, they easily made room for her and considered it a blessing to do so. They never complained about Grandma moving in with us for the last weeks of her life. They made the daily care of Mom easier because of their love and support.

x

Prologue

Who comes to mind when you think of someone who loved you the most? Several people come to mind including my husband, but my mom sticks out most of all. My mom loved me before I was born, before she ever saw my face. She loved me in my terrible two's and trying three's. She loved me in my tumultuous teens when my hormones were raging or when I had zits popping out on my face. She loved me by disciplining me. She loved me by encouraging me. She loved me by showing me what it looked like to love while she cared for my grandma so Grams could be independent. She was kind to others. She thought of others. She encouraged me to be kind - to be wise with my words. She was there for me when my dad (her husband) died. She was there when I graduated from high school and college.

She was there to walk me down the aisle to give me to my husband. She was there when I was so sick and hospitalized while expecting my first born. She was there for the birth of her first grandchild, our first-born son. She moved down to be near her grandchildren when our second child was one, as she put it, "to help Kay with those kids." She was there. She was beloved mom, sister, friend, grandma, and the favorite aunt. When she was dying of cancer, friends and family alike flooded the hospital and then our home for the last weeks of her life. She had at least six visitors a day while she was hospitalized and several per day at our home. She would look at me and say, "Who knew?" or "Who would have thought?" Who would have thought love would make such a difference?

Yes, Mom comes to mind when I think of the person who loved me the most and showed me how to love others, but there is someone who loves me even more—who knew me before I was even created, who drew me to Himself and has been there for me. Oh, yes, my God, He loves me, and He gave me strength for this journey.

~~~~

Death. Though the sudden death of my dad three weeks shy of my sixteenth birthday fractured my world, the death of Mom took me on an unforeseen journey: a journey of tears, time, and treasured memories, a journey of an hour by hour reliance on God. He was my strength for this journey. He still is. To Him be the glory. Soli Deo Gloria (S.D.G.)

Planning the Party

January 2008

"Mom, I am planning a party for your eightieth. When would you like it? The last weekend in February or the first weekend in March?"

Mom's birthday, February 28, fell in between the two, and I thought she would choose the first of March since it was closer. Thankfully, she chose the end of February.

~~~~

Mom's Birthday

February 28, 2008

Feverish with the flu, I vaguely remember hearing my family drive off to pick up Mom for her 80th birthday dinner at her favorite Italian restaurant. Of all the days to be sick, I thought—her 80th birthday. My mind drifted back to her party. All three of her siblings were able to attend—no small fete considering their health. Second born of the four, Mom was the healthy one. Last month, she even helped her sister, Laverne, and brother-in-law, Jerry, pack up their old house and unpack their boxes of stuff into their new townhome. I've heard numerous relatives say, "She has those Nasi genes. I bet she will live as long as her mother." I'm not sure Mom would like to live another twenty years, but I knew I wouldn't mind if she lived to one hundred.

(L to R: Calvin, Clyde, Laverne, & Mom
Mom's 80th Birthday Party - February 23, 2008)

February 29, 2008

Leap-Year Day. Mom came within half an hour of being a leap-year baby. We have had a few on my mom's side who have been born on that day.

I think Jacob, our youngest son, may have come down with the flu. He is running a fever. He was fine last night, so I hope Mom wasn't exposed to it.

~~~~

The Journey Begins

March Madness

March 2, 2008

It's official. The Lukkarilas are succumbing to the virus one by one. Rachel, our youngest daughter, is down for the count. I'm praying Mom won't get it; after all, she's had a flu vaccine. Maybe she won't be stricken with it; she's been sticking close to her apartment a block away because she doesn't want this nasty virus. I am thankful we celebrated her birthday with friends and family last weekend.

~~~~

March 6, 2008

Another one down. Our oldest son, Jimmy, this time. Just when one kid is on the mend, another one comes down with the flu. This could be a long month. I hope Mom won't catch it.

~~~~

The Flu?

March 7, 2008

"I think I'm coming down with it," Mom coughed in response to my inquiry of her health when I called her early this morning.

"Oh no, Mom. Do you have a fever?"

"No, I think there is something wrong with my thermometer. You know how old it is."

Yes, I did. She still had her old mercury thermometer. Mom, a product of the depression and a widow at fifty-one, was frugal with a capital 'F'. Per her request, I picked up some essentials for her—minus a new thermometer.

However, the flu for an octogenarian is nothing to mess with, so I asked her if she wanted to go to the clinic. I should have expected the adamant "NO!" She never liked going to the doctor. In fact, until she moved here to be closer to her grandchildren, she hadn't had an annual physical in years. The only time she consented to see a physician was when she was so sick from a benign ovarian tumor. At that time, the physician admitted her to the hospital directly from the clinic.

When she moved here, I gave her an ultimatum since I didn't want anything like that happening again. The old adage "an ounce of prevention is worth a pound of cure" ran through my mind. Anyway, I told her she could make an appointment for an annual physical, or I could make one for her. She made the appointment and was under the care of a physician for high blood pressure. She continued her yearly check-ups with Dr. Spinner, maybe because he told her she was in great shape for her age—which she was.

Mom

March 8, 2008

Huffing and puffing as she came down her apartment stairs to let me in, Mom handed me her keys. Then I knew she was feeling punk.

"I can take you to urgent care, Mom." We slowly made our way up the stairs to her second-floor apartment.

"I will be all right."

Yeah, she looked it, but I kept my mouth shut and felt her forehead. It seemed cool, but she was coughing quite a bit.

"What color phlegm are you coughing up—clear, yellow, green? Any blood?" I probed. She thought clear or white. Hmmm. Well that didn't help. Yellow or green seemed to indicate an infection. Clear for me usually meant allergies.

There's a fine line when dealing with elderly parents. At what point should I overrule her and tell her I am taking her in or let her decide? She was used to being independent, living on her own, and making her own decisions. She insisted she would be fine. After all, she'd had the flu shot. Not much comfort to me considering how she looked.

~~~~

March 9, 2008

I let myself in to Mom's apartment with the keys she'd handed me the day before. She looked much the same and said she felt much the same, pale and weak. I offered to take her in, but once again, she declined.

"Jimmy's fever was down a little this morning. Maybe you will turn the corner, too," I encouraged as I finished up her dishes. Strangely, it appeared she wasn't running a fever.

~~~~

Doctor's Orders

March 10, 2008

Monday morning. 7:45 a.m. "Mom, I am taking Jimmy into the doctor. His fever spiked again. Do you want me to make an appointment for you, too?" Having dealt with many viral infections with my children through the years, I knew the point at which a bacterial infection was added to the viral. Maybe Mom wouldn't feel as if she were imposing since I would be taking Jimmy in too.

"I guess I'd better," Mom breathlessly returned. "I had trouble making it from the bedroom to the kitchen table." Alarm slammed through me.

At the first appointments of the day with different physicians, I ran between the exam rooms for my mom and my son. Jimmy was finished long before Mom and isolated himself in the corner of the waiting room while I dashed to the in-house pharmacy to fill his prescription and hustled back for the latest update on Mom. The X-rays revealed fluid on the right lung. By Dr. Spinner's orders, we were to head straight to the hospital. "Once again," I thought, "directly from the clinic to the hospital."

"Will you stop by my apartment for an overnight bag?" Mom requested as I started for home to drop off Jimmy.

"Doctor's orders, Mom. I am supposed to take you right to the hospital. They are expecting you."

"I know, but it won't take long. You can get my toothbrush and extra clothes."

Her apartment was on the way to our house, and since I had to stop briefly at home to drop off Jimmy, I turned into the parking lot of her apartment building.

"Mom, I'll grab what you need and be right back," I told her as I parked the car.

"While you are up there will you do my dishes? I didn't get them done last night or this morning," she piped up when I was half-way out of the car.

"Seriously, Mom? No. No way! I was told to go straight to the hospital. I was not even supposed to stop! NO!" I hurried up to her apartment and glanced in the kitchen sink at the three dirty dishes. Shaking my head, I made my way to her bedroom to throw some of what she had deemed essentials into her red overnight bag.

"I will do your dishes when I get back, okay?" I informed Mom as I climbed back in the car. Always a neatnik, she visibly relaxed knowing the dishes would be done.

Stopping briefly at my house to drop off Jimmy, I quickly called my sister's home and cell phones and left messages that Dr. Spinner had ordered Mom to be hospitalized.

Once at the hospital, she was admitted into a room with a huge yellow "caution" sign, indicating she was contagious. Preliminary indications were that she had the

14

flu complicated by pneumonia. Because of the large amount of fluid in her right lung, doctors removed the fluid, x-rayed her lungs again, and began an IV with antibiotics in it.

Later that afternoon, as her doctor reviewed the second X-ray with me, I asked him about the spot that showed up on her right lung, previously hidden by the fluid.

"That is what we're going to find out." The doctor ordered a biopsy and a CAT scan.

I had an inkling that this was not just the flu.

~~~~~

16

The Diagnosis

March 13, 2008

Advocate. Liaison. Informer. My role as daughter had changed just as this day had changed my life forever. The diagnosis: malignant adeno carcinoma in the lungs, which had metastasized to the bones and liver. Stage 4. Terminal. Yucky cancer. Stupid cancer. I asked how long. Silence. I know doctors don't like to give estimates, but I wanted to know how much time Mom had left.

"A year? A few months? Weeks?" I persisted.

"I wouldn't say a year. Maybe a few months." The doctor continued, "The oncologist will be stopping by later to discuss treatment."

After asking if we had any more questions, he left. I broke down.

"It'll be all right, Kay." Dry-eyed, Mom hugged me and continued, "I'm ready to go."

Well, she may be ready to go, but I was not ready for her to go. The phone rang after I had barely contained my tears. I answered. At the sound of my husband, Chuck's voice, I burst into tears again and gasped for air between sobs.

"Give me that phone," ordered Mom. She calmly informed him of the diagnosis and talked with him until I was able to control myself long enough to make arrangements to meet him at home and return later that evening. He was hesitant to let me drive home. I said I'd be okay.

"Are you okay to drive?" I nodded to Mom's question, hugged her goodbye, and prayed it was true.

Sniffing back tears, I walked down the hall, snagged a nurse, and asked to use a phone. I called my sister and broke down again while informing her of Mom's death sentence. Stupid cancer.

After I hung up, a nurse who had overheard my conversation said, "I am so sorry."

"Thank you," I mumbled and somehow found my way to the car.

Sitting in the driver's seat, my heart breaking and tears streaming, I cried out in anguish to God. Minutes ticked by before I felt confident enough to drive. I remember every second of that drive home.

Lord, please get me home. Another mile. Hold on. Almost there. By the time I had arrived home, my husband was there with open arms waiting to comfort me. My twenty-minute drive home took longer than his forty-minute one.

The task of informing Mom's three siblings fell to me. To say that they were shocked upon hearing the news would be an understatement. I kept the details brief. My Aunt Laverne broke down and sobbed so hard that I ended up calling my cousin, David, to inform him not only of the diagnosis, but also of his mom's reaction as well.

~~~~

Later that afternoon, I arrived back at Mom's hospital room with my husband and was shocked to find a "Contagious" sign plastered on the door and another patient, who had just been admitted, in the other bed—a lady with the upper respiratory flu! Panic coursed through me as I did an about-face and pushed through the door.

"What?" I confronted the nurse coming toward her room and pointed at the door. "You can't put someone who has the flu in with my mom! She has lung cancer. She doesn't have the flu! She can't be exposed to it!"

"I know. I tried to tell them that," she replied.

"Well, this can't happen! You need to find a different room for her!" Distress laced my voice as I followed her down the hall. I know the nurse was concerned as well and apparently had been trying to relocate Mom to a different room, but I was the advocate at this point. I was not stopping until Mom was moved, or I would move her myself! She was not going to stay in a room with someone who actually had the flu.

"You are right," the nurse decided. She hustled back into the room and moved Mom to a private room.

We barely had time to greet each other, when the oncologist blew in and started explaining the proposed treatment, which would begin the next day.

"I don't want any treatment," Mom, with her mouth pursed stubbornly, informed me as soon as the doctor hustled out.

"I've lived a good life. Your dad is gone. I don't want to spend what time I have left sick."

"Okay. Why didn't you say that when the doctor was here?" She didn't answer, but she was not one for direct confrontation, and I knew there was no changing her mind. Amiable as she was, when Mom decided something, the Finnish "sisu" kicked in, and a room full of elephants couldn't sway her.

This "sisu" gave her the forbearance to receive her numerous visitors, for she not only was Mom and Grandma, but she was also sister, Auntie Loraine, friend, cousin, teacher, and social butterfly. Every day at the hospital, at least a half-dozen friends or relatives came to visit. Some days the count was over twenty! Thankfully a friend of ours, Brent Johnson, suggested we start a *Caring Bridge®* site[1] to update people. Those entries are in bold.

~~~~

Unexpected Journey

On March 13, 2008, Loraine was diagnosed with malignant adeno carcinoma. The cancer is in her lungs as well as her bones, liver and esophagus. Because of her age, the type of cancer and the wishes of my mom, she will not be having chemo, radiation, or surgery. She had a procedure to keep the right lung from filling up with fluid. She has had no pain or any symptoms other than she was hospitalized a week ago because they thought she had pneumonia. She is now in hospice care at home.

~~~~

If the impact my mom had on people could be measured by the number of people who came to visit her in the hospital and at home during her illness, then the impact was stunning. Whether they visited or wrote well-wishes on her *Caring Bridge*® site, family and friends expressed their love and appreciation for the impact she'd had on their lives. She, too, was surprised as she repeated many times during those last weeks, "Who would have thought?" Kind, caring, thoughtful. That is who she was. After her death, I found a notecard with the birthdays of not only her grandchildren but also her grandnieces and grandnephews. That is how she remembered all those birthdays.

~~~~

The Retreat

March 15, 2008 at *A Day Away Women's Retreat in Becker*

Strength for the Journey. It started out as the title for our church's *A Day Away* Women's Retreat; I was on the planning team. When we started planning almost a year earlier, I thought, "Well, that's great, but it doesn't apply to me." What arrogance! Little did I know that the message would be so applicable for me and at a time when I needed it the most.

Strength for the Journey

"Don't worry that you're not strong enough before you begin. It is in the journey that God makes you strong."

How true! The speaker, Marilyn Wallberg, was a former flight attendant. Toward the end of the day, we all had a "baggage ticket" to fill out. On it, we were to list what was hindering our journey, and then we were to go place it in a box to be given to Jesus. FEAR—that was my hindrance. Though I filled out the ticket immediately, I sat in my chair not wanting to release it. I feared life without my mom. She was an integral part of my life. She understood me, loved me. She had lived two blocks from me for the last thirteen years. The reason she moved down was to "help Kay with those kids." The fear was profound. Releasing it meant releasing my mom. Nope. Not ready. On a stifled sob, I wearily dropped the baggage ticket into the box, releasing the fear to God. After releasing it, I knew such peace. I knew with the Lord I would have strength for the journey. The Scripture verse for the retreat was Isaiah 58:11 (KJV): *"The Lord shall guide thee continually and satisfy thy soul."* He guided me every step of the journey. He was my strength for this journey. He is my strength today. May you find the Lord to be your strength in the trials you face on this journey of life.

24

Hospice at Home

March 21, 2008 - 9:44 p.m.

Mom is having a better day today. She has eaten more today than she has for the last several days. Blessings to my Aunt Laverne as she is staying with Mom since she cannot be alone yet. We also met with the hospice people this afternoon, and they were extremely helpful.

Thanks to all of you who came to visit her in the hospital, called her or sent her cards. She so enjoyed it, and it made the time go much faster for her. Thank you also to my prayer warriors all over the state and country for lifting her up in prayer. Please pray that Mom will continue to gain her strength, as she wants to spend a little more time with all her grandchildren. Please continue to pray for us as well. As many of you know, I attended a retreat March 15th entitled Strength for the Journey. I no longer fear losing my mom. God has given me joy and peace. Yes, I'm still sad - you know moms are supposed to live to be one hundred, just like my grandma!

My maternal great-grandmother lived to be ninety-four and my maternal grandmother, Lili, lived three weeks shy of her 100th birthday. So, longevity is in the genes. Mom's sister-in-law, Lou Ann, thought Mom would out-live all three of her siblings. She wasn't the only one who thought this.

Mom's only sister, Laverne, though riddled with arthritis, drove down to stay with Mom for a few days to help her get back on her feet. Though she was the main caregiver for her husband, my Uncle Jerry, who had Lewy Body disease, she left him in the care of their oldest grandchild,

Peter. Mom had done so much for Laverne in helping her with recovery from her many surgeries that she felt it was the least she could do.

"Your mom can't stay here by herself," Auntie Laverne informed me when I delivered the mail and some groceries.

"She can't?" I knew the stay at the hospital had weakened her, because the first day when they thought she had pneumonia, she was put on antibiotics, which gave her a harsh case of "Montezuma's Revenge."

"No, she hasn't been feeling well for a while."

"How do you know?"

"Things aren't up to her usual standard."

Mom had always been extremely meticulous and organized in her house keeping. Upon going through her papers and bills, Auntie Laverne had discovered things were not as neat and precise as they had been. Mom had let things go but had covered up nicely by having all things clean and tidy on the surface. I wonder how many times we do that with people around us. Cover things up, put on a fake smile and say everything is fine, when in reality, we are dying from the stress of it all.

Thinking this might be the case, our family had already discussed the possibility of Mom moving in with us, but I thought we would have a few more weeks to make preparations. No problem, we would make room for her at our house as planned. Sarah, our oldest daughter, would move back in with her sister, Rachel, and Mom would have Sarah's room. Providentially, we had finished our basement

26

five months prior and the boys, who had previously occupied Sarah's room, already resided downstairs.

~~~~

March 24, 2008 - 9:58 a.m.

Grandma Loraine,

You are very special to me. I love you, and I am praying for you. I am glad to give up my room for you.

Love,
Sarah

Mom and Sarah

Since Mom had so many friends and oodles of relatives, I journaled the days on the *Caring Bridge*® site. All those entries are in bold. Many friends and family surrounded us with love and prayers, either in person or across the miles. We were so blessed by the encouraging words, prayers and general well-wishes that I included some of those entries as well, although some were edited for space. They all were printed and read daily to my mom.

~~~~

Wanda Kaufmann | March 21, 2008

Loraine,

Our prayers are with you. Bill and I pray for peace with you and all of your family. I really enjoyed visiting with you last week. It was wonderful to hear about some of your teaching experiences and learning more about your life. I will come visit you again soon. Hopefully tomorrow.

Lots of Love and Prayers.

Wanda

March 23, 2008

Easter Sunday. Since Mom's diagnosis, special days are bittersweet. We celebrate the risen Lord! However, we know that this will be the last Easter we have with Mom. We try to be optimistic by thinking that next Easter, Mom will be singing with the angels, yet we are somewhat melancholy because next year she will be in heaven without us.

Jane Hartmann | March 23, 2008

Kay, it's Easter Sunday... a glorious day to reflect on the power of our God and the amazing things He has in store for us—now and in heaven! Our prayers continue to be with you, your mom, and your family. Have a blessed Easter!

Love,

Jane and Bill

God provided strength for the journey through the many people who lifted us up in prayer, through the many meals that friends, neighbors, and church family provided, and through the encouragement and love that many people expressed in the guestbook entries on the *Caring Bridge®* site. Some of those entries also mentioned the impact that my mom had on people's lives.

~~~~

Joel & Patti Friday | March 24, 2008

Hi Loraine,

I'm so sorry to hear that you're not feeling well now. It was so good to see you last week; it hardly seemed like you were sick. I guess I've never said thank you for all you've done and meant to me over the years. You've been such a blessing to me and to so many others. You will be greatly missed. I will be praying for you, Mary, Kay, and their families.

God Bless you,

Patti

~~~~

Janet Krogstad | March 24, 2008

Kay -

I continue to pray for you, your family and your mom. I just wanted to share a little story with you—I was on my way into work this morning, praying while I was driving, and out of nowhere, a rainbow appeared. It was out just long enough for me to see it, and then it was gone. It was a great wake-up call for me, knowing that even on our down days, God is always listening and with us wherever we go. We love you and will continue praying!!!

Janet Krogstad

~~~~

Jim Ronkainen | March 24, 2008 -10:32 p.m.

Hi, Auntie Loraine

I just wanted to send you a note to let you know how special you are to me. When I was growing up, you were more like a second mom to me than an aunt, and Mary and Kay are really more like sisters than cousins. I deeply cherish the time I've shared with you and the memories I have of you. We are praying for you and for Mary, Kay and their families. I love you!
God's Peace!

Jim (aka Jimmy)

Aunts Swap Duties

March 24, 2008 - 10:01 a.m.

Mom will be seen by the nurse this afternoon. She was very weak yesterday and was gasping for breath when her oxygen tube came off. Friday, the nurse had to turn her oxygen up to 2.5 liters (2.5L). She will be moving into our home on Thursday since she cannot be by herself. My Aunt Laverne and Aunt Joan are swapping duties, so Joan is on her way down to stay with my mom until Thursday. Please pray for Mom to have the strength for her to make it to our house. Please pray for comfort and encouragement for my sister, Mary and her family as well as for my family. Please pray that our children feel free to express their grief and not bury it.

Huge thanks to all my friends & relatives for their visits, calls and support. Praise the Lord that He is with us in this journey. Life without my mom will be sad, but life without my Savior would be unthinkable. He is good - all the time, and in the darkest night, His light will shine.

My Aunt Joan is Mom's sister-in-law on my dad's side. Though more mobile than my Aunt Laverne, Joan, too, limped around with painful knees, but didn't complain.

~~~~

Laverne Ronkainen | March 24, 2008 - 6:04 p.m.

Hi Loraine,

I made it home about 2:30. Stopped at Coborn' s in Mora like you used to do. You were a very good patient for me and I will always treasure the time we had together...the past few days and all the other times we had in our lifetime. You have been the "best" sister I could have ever had and I want you to know I will miss you greatly until I see you again in heaven. We had many great times over the years...our year in LA, our trip to Yellowstone, our trips to Michigan and many other times. Thanks for all the nursing care you have given me with all my surgeries. I appreciated each time and hope I was of some comfort to you in this time of your illness.

God Bless you and God's Peace.

Love,

Laverne

~~~~

Since Mom and Laverne had only lived ten minutes apart while Mom lived in Esko, Minnesota, they shared so much of life as adults and were as close as any sisters I've known.

~~~~

Laverne Ronkainen | March 25, 2008

Hi Loraine,

I'm recuperating today from the tiredness I felt when I got home. I hope your day is going well. I'm sure a bath and visits with Joannie, Kay and Mary were refreshing. Thanks again for everything...for all the caring of Jim and David when they were little and the fun we had helping raise each other's "kids", the times we spent at the nursing homes with Mom and Dad as well as all you did for Mom and Dad while they were still at home, and all you did for Anna. And the times we cared for Hattie, Anna and Ruth. There were so many times—I can't list them all... but your caring is a treasure in heaven waiting for you.

Love,

Laverne & Jerry

Nothing Wrong with My Mind!

March 25, 2008 - 6:23 a.m.

My verse for today is found in Isaiah 41:10: *"So do not fear, for I am with you; do not be dismayed, for I am your God. I will strengthen you and help you; I will uphold you with my righteous right hand."*

I pray daily that God would give me the strength to face the day or sometimes the strength to face the next ten minutes. Please pray this for us today. My sister is coming today, and we are meeting with Mom to help her with funeral arrangements.

Many of you have asked how much time she has. Only God knows that for sure, but the nurse said that if you want to come and visit her while she is still able to visit, you should do so while she still can. The physical therapist met with Mom yesterday and instructed her on ways to conserve her energy so she can spend it visiting. (We will be moving her to our house on Thursday, so that day would not be a good day to visit.) The nurse increased her oxygen to 3L and said she could have it higher if she needs it. Mom asked for it to be increased while she was eating.

My mom is very much at peace because she knows someday soon she will be with her Savior. My prayer is that all of you would trust Him too. Then you would have the peace and comfort to know that you will someday see her again. Soli Deo Gloria.

Is it obvious yet that Mom loved people? That is why she became a teacher. She loved people, and she especially loved kids. She rarely had anything negative to say about anyone. When speaking to children, she would get down to their level and talk to them. She never talked baby-talk to any child, not even to her grandchildren. So, when the physical therapist came, I listened to her talk to my mom in a baby-talk voice as if she had no faculties left. At one point, the therapist turned away from Mom, providing her with the opportunity to roll her eyes so I could see. I zipped out of the room to cover my laughter.

As soon as the therapist left, I checked on Mom, and she spouted, "I hate when people do that. There's nothing wrong with my mind." No, there wasn't, but she wouldn't say anything to the therapist.

~~~~

Carol Seibert | March 25, 2008

Dear Loraine,

I cry with sadness as I try to decide which thoughts to put down here... they won't all fit, so here are just a few... you mean so much to me! It is hard to think of letting you go- God knows, if it were up to us, we wouldn't ever let any of our loved ones leave us, would we? I knew you first as the mother of my friends, Mary and Kay, and then I came to think of you as my friend. There hasn't been as much time this year as in the past because of teaching full time, but I have thought of you often as I taught. I especially thought often about whether I could convince you to come in and volunteer and help me out! You always were interested in me and my family and my job, and you made me feel special because of that. Your experiences in teaching were fun to talk about, and I treasure the memory of your stories and our laughter when we talked. I have the kitchen angel up on my wall, you know... the one you made of kitchen towels and an ice cream scooper... I think of you when I see it.

May the Lord bless you and keep you...He is holding you in the palm of His hand. Bye for now... I will see you soon.

David & Tammy Ronkainen | March 25, 2008 - 4:32 p.m.
Loraine:

This is hard—these are usually the kind of things you say at a funeral—but then I think—this is so much better—we can still tell you when you can hear and appreciate the words.

I just wanted to let you know how much we love you. I echo Jim's thoughts that you were more like a second mom than just an aunt, and yes, Mary and Kay were like sisters to me, too (bossy ones I remember :>)).

I remember going out to Finlandia in the summers, traveling to Alaska on the adventure of a lifetime, how much I love canned venison (first tasted it on that Alaska trip), Friday night sauna (complete with Club crackers and raspberry Vitasun and sometimes Schwan's® chocolate chip ice cream), going out to Charlie's and Anna's for sauna with you, berry picking up the Shore, and so many more memories. Just today, I recalled as a little boy going with you, Herman, Kay and Jim to the car dealership in Cloquet when you were getting a new car, getting out of the old car you were trading in, and saying out loud (probably in front of the salesman) how it's good you're getting rid of the noisy car and getting a new one. Sorry about that one—hope the deal was done before we got there. I also really appreciated your recent help in moving my folks—your moral support was as great as all the work you did.

I'm saddened that you're leaving us so soon—I guess I always had in mind that you were Lili Rengo's daughter, and you were going to hit 100 and we'd have 20 more

40

years to visit—but God tells us our thoughts aren't His thoughts—and life goes on.

The great consolation is that you're going home to be with Jesus, and I know we'll see each other again on the other side of the grave—we have Hope!

The kids were all sad when we shared the news. They've all come to appreciate Auntie Loraine—your kindness— your game playing with them at Grandpa & Grandma's house (you never did win—did you?), the rummage sale golf balls, the list goes on. Even Adam—the boy who would "lock up" when we'd arrive at G&G house and Auntie Loraine's car was there—he was sad as we left your birthday party at Kay's a few weeks back and told us when we got home that he wanted to go back to Auntie Loraine's birthday again.

We're continuing to pray for God's hand of mercy and bountiful grace for you, Kay & Mary and families—God's Peace.

Love,

David & Tammy

Pete, Tim, Matt, Josh, Eli, Seth, Abby, Luke, Adam, & Isaiah

Nancy Kyllonen | March 26, 2008

Dear Loraine,

You have been in our thoughts and prayers—remembering so many memories, the Alaska trip, camping, etc. And also exchanging tidbits of our loving grandkids!! One never knows what will happen in our lives from day to day. God will take care of you and your family. Great is His loving arms that enfolds us in when it is most needed.

Love & God's Precious Peace,

Billy & Nancy

Herman & Loraine on Alaska Trip
Celebrating their 25th Wedding Anniversary

Rest

March 26, 2008 - 7:47 a.m.

"Come to Me, all you who are weary and burdened, and I will give you rest" (Matthew 11:28).

My friend, Karol-Rae, has been praying that Psalm 23 would become very real to me. This psalm has become even dearer to me as I've been studying it and reading "Traveling Light" by Max Lucado.[2] My Shepherd has provided me with rest:

- Rest from weariness because He makes me lie down.
- Rest from worry because He leads me.
- Rest from hopelessness because He restores my soul.
- Rest from the shadow of death because He walks me through it.
- Rest from the shadow of grief because He guides me.
- Rest from fear because He comforts me.

May you find true rest in Him.

Please pray for the move tomorrow. My Aunt Laverne suggested I ask the fire department to help move my mom. So I talked with our neighbor Doug, the Assistant Fire Chief, and they are going to carry Mom down the stairs and then back up the stairs in our house. This is a huge answer to prayer since Mom was not looking forward to tackling a flight of stairs. Please also pray that the cancer not go into her brain, which usually happens with this type of cancer. We are also praying that she will not suffer. Praise the Lord that she is not feeling any pain. Thank you all for your prayers. I could feel them yesterday while we were planning her funeral. (I highly recommend planning your own funeral before you die; it is much less stressful than having those left behind do it in the midst of shock and grief.) S.D.G.

David & Tammy Ronkainen | March 26, 2008

Dearest Loraine,

I've been thinking how best to put into words what you mean to me. I don't know that I can adequately express just how special a lady you are. Thank you for welcoming me into your family for the past 22+ years. Thank you for the love you have shared with all of my kids as well as the love you have shown me. I think you know that even down to the littlest one, all of our kids have enjoyed spending time playing with Auntie 'Raine. You're a kind and giving woman, and none of that has gone unnoticed. I feel so blessed to have had the privilege of knowing and loving you. I am also ever so thankful that this good-bye will not be a forever one. It's just "So long, I'll see you in Glory." You will never be far from my thoughts and you will always hold a special place in my heart. As you've been going through this difficult time in preparation for your journey, I have been struck by how powerful "God's Peace" is. I pray God's peace and comfort for you as well as your precious family during this time. If there is an upside to all of this, it's that we get the opportunity to tell you things that might not otherwise get said.

Thank you, for blessing my life with yours.

Tammy

Moving Day

March 27, 2008 - 6:41 a.m.

"I can do all things through Him who strengthens me" (Philippians 4:13 NASB).

Today is moving day. Please pray that it all goes well, and it not be hard on my mom. She has been a real trooper through all of this, although it is difficult for her to be on the receiving end of having everything done for her.

Yesterday, she asked that her oxygen be moved up. It is now at 4L. Maximum level is 5L and she was already at that when she continued to complain of not having enough breath while she was sitting down to eat. We then discovered she had sat on her air hose and had cut off her air supply. :) That was good for a few laughs.

The nurse saw her yesterday and told us if she is up at 5L and having difficulty, then there is a medicine we can give her that will go to the same receptor sites in the brain that are for breathing and help them relax so she doesn't feel oxygen deprived.

Praise God that Mom continues to be pain free. May He continue to be glorified through all this.

Joyce Luttinen | March 27, 2008

Dear Loraine,

We're thinking of you and hoping your move goes well for you today. We were so sad to hear this news but glad you're surrounded by your loving family, and I hope you know so many of us are also praying for you. What a comfort it is to be "Safe in the arms of Jesus" through all this.

Love and God's Peace,

Joyce and Ken Luttinen

Joel & Patti Friday | March 27, 2008

Hi Loraine,

I read your guestbook. I love reading the things people write; it brings back memories. It's obvious you are loved. It's good to hear you are still laughing. I can just picture you all when you figured out the plugged air hose. I also was reading David's story about when you were buying a new car. I had to laugh. It brought me back to that car you had—that a mouse had died in. Oh, the smell! I remember thinking that this was so not like you, everything at your house was always so clean. Then there was that car. Anyways, I hope and pray that your day will go well, and that your time at Kay 's will be a blessing to you all.

Love,

Patti

~~~~

Todd Wuollet | March 27, 2008 - 2:06 p.m.

Auntie Loraine,

Memories

The first memories that come to mind were all of the Christmas Eve gatherings at the Wuollet houses. The presents were plenty but not expensive, but the price in each package included thoughtfulness and the time searching for just the right game, puzzle or toy. If laughter were the price of admission to such grand affairs, winning the Minnesota Power Ball may enable one to buy a ticket. Music was also a big part of these parties, with guitars, pianos and strong voices. Last but not least was the food. It was a simple fair by design as to not tax the host and distract them from all of the fun.

First was the singing of the Christmas Carols. Marv would know everyone's favorite and pluck them out on his guitar, one by one. My dad would follow along, and years later, I would try to best my uncle, but not quite. Uncle Martin was there off and on and would add his second tenor voice and guitar. The piano came years later, and the gathering was complete. Having a father, mother and all my uncles as musicians caused me to pick up the guitar and learn to play it to the best of my ability. I am forever grateful for their intuitive sense of music. It warms my heart to know my gift of music made you smile on more than one occasion.

The gifts I gave you were small pieces of silver in the shape of spoons, marking the places I have visited in the world. Your gift to me has been your laughter, your generous spirit and wisdom. You are a model to follow, living without complaint and looking for the bright side of all situations in life. It is a tribute to your Finnish descent. The most vivid memory I have of Uncle Herman is his big smile and shining eyes behind those thick horned-rimmed glasses. We are all at different points in our journey, and I can only pray for God's will to be done and give thanks for the grace that He shows all of us.

I Love You.

Todd

Dena Ryttie | March 27, 2008

Hi Loraine,

I was sad to hear about your illness, but my soul rejoices that your journey's end will be in Heaven with your loved ones. May God comfort you and your family during this time. I leave you now in God's Peace and His loving care and know that I will see you—if not on this earth, then we'll meet again in Heaven!

Jumalan Rauhan! (God's Peace)

Dena Ryttie

Conserving Energy

March 28, 2008 - 7:41 p.m.

"Jesus wept." (John 11:35).

Thank you all for your prayers. The move went well. Special thanks to Doug Kolbinger and his friend from the Becker Fire Department who carried Mom down the stairs of her apartment and back up the stairs in our house, to Bill Kaufmann and Gene Tiegland for helping us move my mom, and to Wendy Jundt for providing us with supper after an exhausting day. We were so blessed by you.

Mom was weaker today. She commented that it was such a long way from her bedroom to the living room. She was quite out of breath by the time she got there.

Lesa, the nurse, came today, and I expressed my concerns. I am seeing an increase in weakness every day. Lesa said to increase her oxygen to 5L when mom is walking or eating. Her lungs are clear of fluid, but there is decreased air flow in them. The nurse also confirmed my suspicions that time is running out fairly quickly. She did not think my mom would live longer than a month. We are doing things to conserve the remaining energy she has so she can visit. When my mom saw Lesa, Mom informed her, "My nephew, Jim, came to visit me all the way from Kentucky." She was so thrilled, and it made her feel very special and loved that he would fly in one day, see her the next day, and fly back right after that.

Clyde and Lou Ann came to visit this afternoon as well. She appreciates all the visitors, calls, cards and messages on the guestbook. I print up the messages every day so she can read them. Thank you for showing her how much you love her. If you are planning to visit her while she still can talk, I would do so soon. Please pray very specifically that

1. She not have air hunger.
2. She not die on Rachel's birthday (April 4).
3. She not have pain or linger long.

God continues to provide grace for the moment. All the glory goes to Him.

~~~~

March 28, 2008 - 12:30 p.m.

Dear Loraine,

God's Peace and all my love...

Give regards to my mom and grandparents and all the other believers in heaven. Dad & I will miss you, but know you will be in a better place, where there is no pain or suffering but only "Joy Immense in heaven and precious rapture ever!"

Love and God's Peace,

Cal & Carolyn.

~~~~

March 28, 2008

MEMORIES TOO!

Hi Auntie,

I see that Todd wrote some of the things I was thinking of the other night after a long talk with Mary. He was so right about our Christmas Eve celebrations and the love that went into them—all the little presents, the singing, the food. Just being together as a family was really what it was all about. There are so many things to say and so hard to say them.

I was thinking also of the other times that we spent together. Not so much with all the family, but just ours and yours and the camping trips we used to take. We would go to Crescent Lake or maybe to Fall lake in Ely. Dad and Mom would make sure we had everything, especially the canoe, and of course, Uncle Herm would bring his boat. So many times that canoe would go on great adventures to uncharted islands or some small stream that we (Mary, Marty, and I) would find as we paddled around the lake. Then there were those times we would find ourselves in trouble on the wrong side of the lake in bad weather that came up as it often does in Minnesota. We would wonder how we were going to make it back when... What's that sound? The soft roar of an outboard motor and around the bend would come Uncle Herm and my Dad always there when we needed them most. You and Mom would be waiting impatiently at the camp site for our safe return, always with a hug and kiss, and some strong words of admonishment. Never without love! Those were the days.

The best memory I have though is of a time at Fall lake. It is a story often told around a supper table for that is where it took place—a simple table of wood in a small camp site. You had invited us to share dinner that evening and had told Mom you had plenty for everyone. As you and yours were never big eaters, Mom grabbed the bread and peanut butter and some other odds and ends, just to help out. Your stew (mojakka, am I close?) was excellent, served in 2qt sauce pan. It never made it to Mom that night as it was passed around the table. A day I will never forget and so often share with others. You so often stated, "My, how those boys can eat!"

The years have gone by, but the memories never fade. The love shared, the laughter, the smiles, and the little things remembered. Thank you for all you have ever been. God bless you Auntie. I am going to miss you!

All my love, Jut (Jodie Wuollet)

Jim Ronkainen | April 4, 2008 - regarding his March 28th visit

Dear Auntie Loraine,

I do my best to keep track of you via the *CaringBridge®* website—it's not the same as being there, but it is the best we can do for now.

I wanted to let you know how much I enjoyed my visit with you last Friday. Saying goodbye is difficult, but when we remember it is only goodbye for now, it takes a little of the sting out of it.

We have lots of memories that we've shared throughout my life. I tell our kids stories every night before they go to bed about "when I was a little boy". One of the stories I shared with the kids one evening just before we found out you were sick was when they put in the sewer along Ridge Road. I know that it doesn't sound like that impressive of an item, but for an 8-year-old boy, it doesn't get much better than bulldozers, backhoes, and track hoes, in the road no less right in front of the house! We must have driven you crazy that day! Your memory will live on with us as long as the stories are told and retold (and that will just have to do until we see you again in heaven).

We continue to pray for you and for Kay and Mary and their families.

God's Peace!

Love, Jim

The Toothbrush

March 29, 2008 - 9:45 p.m.

"For our citizenship is in heaven, from which also we eagerly wait for a Savior, the Lord Jesus Christ; who will transform the body of our humble state..." (Philippians 3:20-21 NASB).

I am eagerly praying for that transformation of my mom's body. She was even weaker today. I wheeled her where she wanted to go so she could conserve her energy for her many visitors. She only tells me what she needs— not what she may want. For instance, sometime during the night, I remembered that I needed to get my mom's toothbrush from her apartment. When I went in to check on her while she was coughing, I mentioned this and she said, "Yes, I've been waiting for it." I wonder how long she would have waited before telling me. We had a few good laughs over that one. She has been a very easy-going patient.

Please continue to pray for all of us. S.D.G.

Brent Johnson | March 30, 2008

Dear Kay,

Thank you for your update. I smiled at the toothbrush story. Just think of things that God is more than willing to give us if we would ask? 😊 As I read your update I thought of the song "I can only imagine" (by Bart Millard)[3] and to know when we get to heaven there is no more sickness and no more wars and no more evil.

What a celebration there will be when your Mom is welcomed into Heaven and she will be free from all this sickness. To be absent from the body is to be present with The Lord.

I pray that God will give the family the Peace that is beyond our Understanding during this time. I don't know what you are going through, but God knows, and only He can meet those needs (as you know). I also pray for your Mom that she will not have a lot of pain, she would be able to share the hope she has with the caregivers and others she comes across during this time.

In the Grip of His Grace,

~~~~~

Don't Lose Heart

March 30, 2008 - 9:30 p.m.

"Therefore we do not lose heart. Though outwardly we are wasting away, yet inwardly we are being renewed day by day. For our light and momentary troubles are achieving for us an eternal glory that far outweighs them all. So we fix our eyes not on what is seen, but on what is unseen. For what is seen is temporary, but what is unseen is eternal" (2 Corinthians 4:16-18).

Praise God that Christ is our hope. I do not lose heart because I know where my mom is headed. After life on this earth is ended for both of us, I will see her again someday. You will too, if you trust in Jesus. Today in church we sang the words, *"On Christ the Solid Rock I stand, all other ground is sinking sand."* There is no fear in death if you are anchored in Christ, the Solid Rock. (Thanks, youth!)

Physically, my mom is about the same as yesterday. We are still wheeling her around, and she told me that Rachel is a better driver than I am. Our walls and doors give testimony to my lack of driving skills—at least I missed the stairs. :)

Today, we were blessed by a visit from Kai and Heidi and their three precious children. Thanks also to Uncle Calvin and Carolyn for sitting and visiting with Mom last night so I could run to the grocery store. Sarah absolutely loves you "Grandpa" Calvin. Thanks to all you who visited, called, wrote or signed the *Caring Bridge®* guest book. There is not room to list you all, but God knows who you are and so do I. You brighten my mom's day.

She tells me all about those who have called while I've been gone.

Thanks to all who are asking not only how Mom is doing, but how I am doing as well. I feel your prayers for strength and encouragement. My immediate family has been a huge blessing to me as well as to my mom. Jimmy stayed with Mom while I went to church this morning. Please pray for my sister, her family and for us as well. Pray as God leads you. He knows best what we need. Soli Deo Gloria.

~~~~

Kristin Salvevold | March 31, 2008

Oh, Kay —

I had NO idea that she was struggling so much and that you are already planning for her funeral. I had tears as I read through your journal entries. I am SO sorry that you are going through this. But I know that you will look for God's hand in it all. What a blessing for your mom to be with your family at this time. Real life tends to be the best teacher, huh? Please know that I am praying for you, my friend. Let me know if you need anything. I don't know your mom well, but I do remember meeting her a few times. What keeps coming to mind is that you have the same relationship with her that I have with my mom—it's something special. God bless you as you make some big memories with her at this time. I love you.

Kristin

Caregiver Plus...

Not only was I Mom's primary care giver 24/7, but I was a wife and also a mom to four children ages six to fifteen. Homeschooling was not put on the back burner, but I did take a leave of absence from any extraneous activities. So while I was taking care of needs (that according to our six-year-old son, Jacob, only Mom could do), my husband kept people updated.

March 31, 2008

"Give thanks to the Lord, for he is good; his love endures forever" **(Psalm 118:1).**

Kay is responding to a needy 6-year-old tonight, therefore, I am trying to help her post this Journal. She is very thankful for supportive friends and relatives in recent days. Heather, Carol, and Wanda helped in ways that she cannot describe.

Loraine had a visit from her nurse today; the only change is that her blood pressure is a little low—106/60.

Loraine fired Kay as the driver of her wheel chair and summoned Rachel to take over (Kay was hitting the walls and doors).

Loraine and her grandson, Jimmy, enjoyed watching the Twins opener tonight (1st victory!).

Thanks for your prayers and notes!

In Christ,

Chuck

Kristin Salvevold | March 31, 2008

Wow—sorry that your driving is so sketchy, Kay. Didn't
Jimmy recently get his license? Is he an acceptable driver?
So glad to get these updates. I hope your 6-year-old trials
are over by tomorrow. His mercies are new everyday—I
remind myself of that often. God is good. Take care!

A Cheerful Heart

April 1, 2008 - 8:19 p.m.

"A cheerful heart is good medicine" Proverbs 17:22.

Mom tricked Rachel and me with the first April Fool's joke of the day. She started a trend that all the kids were trying to top. Mom felt good today—well as good as she can feel. Getting wheeled around conserves her energy so she can visit. She was energized by cousins, Clayton and Brenda, and bother, Clyde and niece, Patti.

Please pray for my sister's family as they have or are coming down with the flu.

Soli Deo Gloria,

Kay

April 2, 2008 - 10:18 p.m.

"Be still, and know that I am God;" Psalm 46:10a.

Not much change with Loraine today. Please pray that she gets a good night sleep.

Rachel had her friend, Rachel, over today, and she had an early birthday party at Chuck E. Cheese's. Kay is exhausted from the running around. Please pray for her to get her rest.

Thanks for all your prayers!

In Christ,

Chuck

The Best Driver

April 3, 2008

I've been meditating on Psalm 63 for the last several days. If you have time, please read all the verses. Verses 7 and 8 describe my last few days. *"Because you are my help, I sing in the shadow of your wings. I cling to you; your right hand upholds me."* Praise God. He does uphold me. I even had time to play the piano!

Mom seems to have stopped the drastic decline and has been somewhat stable. She (as did I) had a good night sleep. Many thanks to Wanda for sitting with my mom so all the kids and I could go out for Rachel's birthday yesterday. (Don't worry, Todd—I am asking for help).

Thanks to Wendy for helping me pack up more of my mom's stuff at her apartment. Thanks to Marty and JoAnn for visiting and getting the hutch, table, and chairs. It's amazing how much we could cram in the truck. Thanks, Carol, for being here and bringing your mom. Mom enjoys your nightly calls, Laverne.

The aide came today, and she also took the front feet holders off the wheelchair. It is amazing how much easier it is to steer and miss the walls and doors. Mom has rated Rachel as the best wheelchair driver. Jim and Sarah are okay, but I am still a distant last.

Thank you all for your calls and prayers. Please continue to pray that my mom will not have air hunger. She gets out of breath at the least bit of activity. S.D.G.

Todd is my first cousin, the third son of my dad's brother, Ed and his wife, Joan. We grew up in the same small township, spent many adventures together since he is only a year older than I am, and attended the same school, so we were often mistaken as siblings. He addressed his concern for my exhaustion—he actually said it best on the *Caring Bridge®* site:

Todd Wuollet | April 3, 2008
1 Thessalonians 1:3: *"We remember before our God and Father your work produced by faith, your labor prompted by love, and your endurance inspired by hope in our Lord Jesus Christ."*

Chuck,

Sometimes we can lose focus in keeping a watchful eye on our health when a labor of love is involved. Loraine and your family are blessed with great love, and I am sure there is help, you only need to ask. Kay is going to need a break now and then.

Kay,

I know how stubborn you can be. Like Paul, this is the thorn in your side. If you need rest, ask for help, and it will be granted. This is God's chance to show His love and caring nature to you. I have fallen into this trap many times myself, and in retrospect, I have missed the chance to spread God's blessings.

Loraine,

I am comforted that things have slowed down and changes are coming more slowly. The time you spend with visitors and family is cherished. Rarely does anyone have a chance to say and do the things they value the most before it is too late. Most of the time we lament with phrases starting with "I wish I would have. I wish I could have." Perhaps we should all live our lives today as if it might be too late. I pray for God's blessings on you and the loved ones around you.

In Christ's Love,

Todd

Todd Wuollet | April 3, 2008

Kay,

When Chuck asked for prayer that both you and your mom get a good night's rest, I got a little concerned. I watched my mom do this all on her own with little or no regard to her own health. I am glad to hear this is not the case with you. I think your mom would also not let it happen.

In Christ's Love,

Todd

Irene Kovala | April 3, 2008

Dear Loraine,

I am touched by the outpouring of love for you in reading these messages. I was so saddened to learn of your illness. You have been such a spark in my life and all the times we visited you, Herm and the girls. I know that God is waiting with open arms for you. "Angels to beckon me...Nearer my God to Thee"

I am thinking of you with love,

Irene Kovala

Heather Bergstedt | April 3, 2008 - 9:25 a.m.

Loraine-

Little did I know when spending time in your home growing up (lots of time....and I'm sure lots of noise from giggly girls!) that you would become, later in life, a treasured neighbor and friend. You were an immense help to us with newborn, Amanda. As new parents, we were reassured knowing you were close by. You will forever be memorialized in our family memories as our girls' prayers always ended with, "God bless Mommy, Daddy...Diana, and Loraine. In Jesus name, Amen." Also, Amanda's rendition of Itsy-Bitsy Spider: "...Down came Loraine, and washed the spider out!" Brian still talks about the time he left his 9-month pregnant wife at home, watching Anne of Green Gables while he went to your house to watch the Twins play in the World Series. We were glad that you could be close to your family when you moved from Esko, but we sure missed you on Ridge Road!
We were saddened at the news of your illness. We continue to pray that you and your family will have strength, comfort, and peace in the days ahead. We just wanted you to know what a special person you have been to all of us.

We love you!

Brian, Heather, Amanda, Megan, and Seth

Air Hunger

April 4, 2008 - 11:18 a.m.

"I have told you these things, so that in me you may have peace. In this world you will have trouble. But take heart! I have overcome the world." In the very next verse, Jesus begins praying to his Father and in John 17:3, Jesus says, *"Now this is eternal life: that they may know you, the only true God, and Jesus Christ, whom you have sent."*

Mom's eternal life has already begun in this world—even in the midst of trouble. She knows Jesus as her Savior. I take comfort in this because she had an episode of trying to catch her breath after she walked the few steps in the bathroom. I had to help her up and out. We just sat in the bathroom and rested until she could catch her breath enough to move to the wheelchair. She was panting and sweating like she had run a mile at full speed. She then sat in the living room and after about half an hour, she felt that she had breath enough to have coffee. Breakfast had to wait for another hour and a half. I asked the nurse and she said the episodes would happen more frequently and it would take longer for her to recover. This is called air hunger. So, we are doing what we can for her comfort. Later this morning, she did manage to sing (albeit breathlessly) "Happy Birthday" to Rachel. Please continue to pray for Mom's comfort as she struggles to breathe. It is difficult to watch her struggle like this so I am praying she not linger, that soon she would dwell in the house of the Lord forever and she will soon see Him face to face.

Soli Deo Gloria

Laverne Ronkainen | April 4, 2008

Loraine,

I read the journal for yesterday and today and am sorry to hear of your breathing problems. I'm sure it is very scary, and I'm praying these episodes will be few and far between.

We will be there tomorrow. Tim has volunteered to drive (I should say Tammy volunteered him) and there was no protest from him... just a grin and look of anticipation. He'll get to chum with Jimmy and his grandparents (Ha!) I hope he doesn't mind.

Stay well and keep looking up!

Love, Laverne & Jerry

Kay,

I pray this time will be a blessing for you. Thank you for your reports via this journal and over the phone. I think I am getting used to the idea of your mom being gone, but all I have to do is read your reports and the letters of tribute and I'm crying even before we've lost her. I wish I was healthier so I could come and take care of her, but I need to heed my limitations and take care of the needs of Jerry. With his lack of vision combined with his Parkinson's, it is a full-time job taking care of him. God gives us strength for the day but not much extra. My mind still goes 100 mph, but my body goes about 20 mph.

Please take care of yourself. I know you are stretched to the limit right now, but before too long this will all be a memory. Thanks for your Bible verses; they are so uplifting, and I treasure each one.

Love, Laverne

74

Memories

April 5, 2008 - 7:20 p.m.

"You have made my days a mere handbreadth; the span of my years is as nothing before you. Each man's life is but a breath" (Psalm 39:5).

Every day with my mom, I am reminded how fleeting life is. I consider these last days we are spending together as a gift from God.

Thanks and praise to God because my mom made it through Rachel's birthday. Mom immensely enjoyed visiting with everyone who came for the birthday party. She was also so pleased to be able to help Ashley furnish her apartment and to support the upcoming sale for Finn Fest. Thank you, Mary, for your help today at the party and after at Mom's apartment. Thanks for your encouragement and prayers. Auntie Laverne, you nearly broke my heart when you sang "God Be with You 'Til We Meet Again" as you said goodbye to my mom. I don't think there was a dry eye in the room.

Thank you, Jim and Dee, for the gift! Yesterday, I was planning a time that I could go out and buy an album for all the pictures that I have been sorting through. You met that need in a very tangible way. We have had many laughs looking at the pictures and telling stories of our growing up years. The story of you getting stuck on the tree branch by the back of your jacket and my dad climbing the snowbank to rescue you came up again today. I also sent more pictures home with your mom today. Thanks, David & Tammy, for sending Tim as the designated grandparents' driver. I'm sure they stayed longer because they didn't have to worry about driving home. Tell Abby and Seth thanks from Rachel.

As we were going out last night for our birthday dinner with Rachel, Mom told Wendy (thanks for staying with her, Wendy) that she used to go along for the birthday dinners. The birthday dinner felt a little empty because Mom was not there to share it with us. These days can go from laughter to tears in short order. (Thank You, Lord, that You know all the tears I cry and that You never waste a hurt.) God alone gets me through my days with strength that only comes from Him. So, thanks to all you who are praying for me and my family. To God alone be the glory! Soli Deo Gloria!

~~~~

Mary Lukkarila | April 5, 2008

Hi, Loraine

We enjoyed our visit with you at Rachel's party. Thank you for the items for the FinnFest Rummage Sale and the books for our Library Book Sale. Ashley is excited about the things she has now for her apartment and thanks you as well. We wish we lived closer so we could be of some help to everyone. You all are in our thoughts and prayers.

Love, Mary

~~~~

Though my mom spoke Finnish, she would often invent words and phrases if she didn't know the Finnish ones. For instance, when she referred to her appendectomy, she said, "Ahpendicitiseea Ohperayseeona." These words and phrases are dubbed "Finglish," and I heard them frequently.

My Aunt Joan would often say, "With Loraine's Finn, anyone can understand it."

~~~~

David & Tammy Ronkainen | April 5, 2008

Hi, Loraine

At supper last night, I was reminded of how instrumental you were in my Finnish education. We had beans as part of the meal, and I remembered a time when we were talking about beans and wondering what the Finnish word for them was. I remember you saying..."Beansies"(for those of you not well versed in Finnish, it's pronounced bean'sees) :) I hope you're teaching your grandkids wonderful "Finglish" words like that in the time you are sharing these days. Got any new ones for me? If I learn enough, I might be ready to take a trip to Finland!

Love,

Tammy (would my name in Finn be "Tammsie"?)

April 6, 2008

This morning before church I was singing the same song we sang today during worship, "Everlasting God," by Brenton Brown & Ken Riley[4]. The words of this song are based on Isaiah 40:28-31: *"The Lord is the everlasting God...He will not grow tired or weary...He gives strength to the weary...Those who hope in the Lord will renew their strength. They will soar on wings like eagles; they will run and not grow weary, they will walk and not be faint."* Praise God that He does not grow weary but gives us strength.

Today, we were blessed by visits from David & Tammy and nine of their children, as well as Joel & Patti and their three girls, and our niece, Heidi. Mom enjoyed her visitors. Jacob announced (when he found out the Ronkainen clan was coming) that he didn't know it would be so fun to have Grandma staying with us. He and Rachel are our social bugs and thrive on company. They get this trait from Grandma Loraine. Thanks, Janet, for the cookies; they were delicious. Belated thanks to Theresa for the cookies as well—they didn't last long either. Thanks Carol—the movie was great! (Happy Birthday, Cousin Jim!)

Mom had a similar episode this evening as she'd had on Friday morning. Thankfully, she was beside her bed and the recovery time wasn't as long, but she was looking a little gray. She asked me to turn the oxygen up, but she was already at 5L. Please pray for a restful night for her. She was coughing a lot more last night. I got up several times to check on her, but it looked like she was sleeping. Thanks to all of you for your prayers. S.D.G.

Karen Gudim | April 7, 2008

I was thinking of your family the whole time we were singing "Everlasting God"! The words we were so perfect, and we continue to pray them for your Mom, your family and the extended family.

Your family is an example of consistency and trust in God and we're thankful for you.

Much love,

Karen

Laverne Ronkainen | April 6, 2008

Hi you all,

This is the third time I am writing this note. I keep getting
thrown out for some reason. Thanks for inviting us to the
party. We made it home in fine style. Tim is a "very good
driver" (much better than Rainman). We stopped at
Tobie's, and I told him about the "real" Tobie's which was
downtown. Just the other day, Janet reminded me of
when we skipped school and hitchhiked to Hinckley to visit
you in your classroom. I have been reformed since then
and do neither of those things anymore.

Take care, Kay...we pray for strength for you. Loraine, we
pray for comfort and no pain. The rest of you, we pray
God's special blessings on you.

Love,

Laverne

April 7, 2008 - 8:54 p.m.

"And the God of all grace, who called you to his eternal glory in Christ, after you have suffered a little while, will himself restore you and make you strong, firm and steadfast. To him be the power for ever and ever. Amen" (1 Peter 5:10-11).

Someday soon God will restore my mom. She will then be home with her Savior, and she will have no more trouble breathing.

Today was not a good day for my mom. She struggled for breath even while eating. The nurse checked her, and Mom once again has fluid in her lungs. She is now on a diuretic and also another medicine to help with air hunger. Thanks, Wanda, for being here for me and for both you and Bill visiting tonight. I am blessed to have you as my friends. Please pray that my mom will not linger long. It is very hard to see her suffer. I am reminiscing about this time last year when we were all (my mom and Chuck's mom included) vacationing in San Antonio. How quickly things can change. S.D.G.

Yes, this time last year we were in Texas. My husband and I took both of our moms along knowing they would enjoy the time with their grandkids, and since we had buried Chuck's dad in January of last year, Chuck's mom, Ida, needed a retreat as well. So, dealing with another imminent death of another parent a little over a year later was added stress—especially for the grandkids.

Mary Lukkarila | April 7, 2008

I found this poem, which I thought I would share:

Jesus Will Be There
Though darker, rougher, grows the way,
And cares press harder day by day,
And nothing satisfies.
The promise sure before me lies
Of that blest place beyond the skies
Where Jesus waits for me.
With sight too dim to visualize
The scene, though spread before my eyes,
I know it will be fair;
Eye hath not seen, ear hath not heard,
The things that are for us prepared,
But Jesus will be there.

~Selected (Author Unknown)

The one verse that always comes to my mind when the
going gets rough is the promise we have been given:

"Lo, I am with you always, even unto the end of the world"
(Matthew 28:20 KJV).

Love, Mary

His Ways

April 8, 2008 - 7:56 a.m.

Isaiah 55:8: *"For my thoughts are not your thoughts, neither are your ways my ways declares the Lord."*

This is how I felt when I woke up. I was struggling with His way. I do not fear letting go of my mom, I just don't want to let go. However, as I continued reading the rest of chapter 55, I know why God's ways are higher than ours. He has the big picture. He knows what awaits my mom. My sister is coming today. Please pray that we all say the things we need to say and that we tell my mom that she can go. For His Glory, alone.

Jane Hartmann | April 8, 2008

Dear Kay,

I continued to keep you, your Mom and your family in prayer. May God continue to guide you in His Word and give you peace.

Love, Jane Hartmann

Family

April 9, 2008 - 9:49 a.m.

"Let us fix our eyes on Jesus, the author and perfecter of our faith who for the joy set before him endured the cross, scorning its shame, and sat down at the right hand of the throne of God. Consider him who endured such opposition from sinful men, so that you will not grow weary and lose heart" (Hebrews 12:2-3).

I thought this verse appropriate for today. My eyes need to be fixed on Jesus. Mom is growing weaker. She even struggles to sit on the side of the bed, so she decided to stay in bed today. She fell back to sleep before she could have her coffee or breakfast. And Jacob, our six-year-old, woke up with a fever. I feel like I am riding a rollercoaster, and it is not even noon.

Thanks to Uncle Calvin and Carolyn for spending last evening with Mom, so Chuck and I could run our errands. Thanks to Bill for his spur of the moment help. Thanks for dinner, Ida. It was great to see you, Mary and Ashley. Thanks for making the meatloaf for the kids, Theresa.

Uncle Clyde, Patti, Uncle Ed and Aunt Joan are coming to see my mom. My friend, Wendy, is bringing supper for us tonight and is arranging for several more meals. I am going to spend my day loving Mom (she does not require a lot of care as she sleeps more now) and caring for Jacob. Thanks to all you prayer warriors. Please pray that no one else gets sick and that this virus be short-lived. For His Glory, alone.

Uncle Calvin is my mom's older brother. With only twenty-one months between them, they are quite close. Throughout the years we have heard many adventures of "those Rengo kids." By the grace of God, they survived their childhood. While living in Meadowlands near the railroad tracks, Calvin, at the age of four, saved my mom from getting hit by the train when he tackled her just before the railroad tracks and sat on her until the train passed. He always said that he was so scared because they were so close to the train, and Mom was thrashing under him.

Aunt Laverne is my mom's younger sister by five years. During my childhood years, our family lived in Esko, Minnesota, while Laverne, her husband Jerry, and their two kids, Jim and David, lived about ten minutes away near Nopeming, Minnesota. Jim is several years older than I am, and David is only a few months older so we spent a lot of time together.

Uncle Clyde is my mom's younger brother by nine years. My mom taught him how to read, so her teaching career began at a young age. Clyde lost his first wife when he was thirty and his son, Scott was eight and his daughter, Patti was seven. I spent a lot of my growing up years with my cousin, Patti, while Scott stayed with Jim and David.

My Uncle Ed is one of my dad's younger brothers. He and his wife Joan and their three boys, Marty, Jodie, and Todd, lived a few miles away from our house in Esko. Since Todd was only a year older than I, his brother Marty a year younger than my sister, and Jodie a few years younger than Marty, we spent many hours together, too.

Laverne Ronkainen | April 10, 2008 - 7:14 a.m.

Loraine,

Good morning! And it is a good morning that the Lord has made. I was thinking of you in the middle of the night in my wakefulness. I talked to Ruth Johnson finally. She was so surprised to hear of your illness and reminisced of your teaching days saying what a wonderful teacher you were. She admired the way you could take over any class and settle the kids down and actually "teach" them something, which was difficult for many subs. We had a nice visit and she sends her greetings to you.

I pray that today is better than yesterday for you. Know that we love you and think of you always. We know God will take care of you. Jerry has been very sad and sends his love, too.

Love, Laverne

Karol Rae Rokala | April 10, 2008

Dear Kay,

Words cannot express my thoughts to you adequately. I wish I could come to see you. It must be incredibly difficult to balance the roles of daughter and mother (as well as wife) when everyone needs you. I heard a message after my grandma died in February about how we can have joy amidst the grief. It was a timely message and I have shared it with several people. The verses that really describe it well are found in 2 Corinthians 4:8-9 (NASB): "We are afflicted (grief) in every way but not crushed (joy), perplexed (grief) but not despairing (joy), persecuted (grief) but not forsaken (joy); struck down (grief), but not destroyed (grief)" [author translation]. I felt these verses really helped me understand how we can be grieving, but not lacking in joy because of Jesus in our lives. We mourn, but not as the world does without hope. I will close with the ending verses of the same chapter,

"Therefore we do not lose heart, but through our outer man is decaying, yet our inner man is being renewed day by day. For momentary, light affliction is producing for us an eternal weight of glory far beyond all comparison, while we look not at the things which are seen, but at the things which are not seen; for the things which are seen are temporal, but the things which are not seen are eternal" (2 Corinthians 4:16-18 NASB).

We love you and pray for strength in the midst of this trial.

April 10, 2008 - 3:49 p.m.

"My grace is sufficient for you..." (2 Corinthians 12:9).

Mom looked a little grayer today. The nurse came and took her vitals. Mom's oxygen level was 86 percent and she was at 5L. Her pulse was up to 113, but her BP (blood pressure) was normal at 110/70. She still has fluid on her lungs, but it is no worse than on Monday. The nurse wants me to give Mom's air hunger meds to her three times daily.

My friend Carol and I sang some of my mom's favorite hymns and songs to her. She even breathlessly sang along when both of us botched the melody on one of the verses of a song. Carol is coming tonight to sing with us again.

Jacob's fever was short-lived, and he seems to be back to normal. (Thank you for praying for him.) He missed his ten minutes alone time with Grandma yesterday, and he usually has so much to say that he informed all of us that ten minutes was not enough time because he still had more to say. My mom often says, with a smile, that Jacob talks as much as her mother used to.

Thanks to all you who visit, call, send cards or sign the guestbook. She enjoys hearing from you. Praise the Lord that the disease is not affecting her mind at all. To God alone be the glory.

My maternal grandmother, Lili Kathryn Nasi Rengo, was indeed a talker. She had a sweet disposition, a mind like a steel trap, and everything she cooked or baked tasted exquisite. Fluent in Finnish and English, she was always learning new things. I believe she would have had a computer if she had lived when they were common to have.

89

Evie Luttinen | April 10, 2008

Loraine,

You brought a smile to my face today after I read Kay's entry that you said your grandson talks almost as much as your mother did! That brought back memories...thanks! It's so great he has these special moments with his grandmother.

Love and Jumalan Rauhaan,

Evie

L to R: Mom, Clyde, Laverne, Calvin with their mother, Lili – seated.

Howard Rengo | April 10, 2008

Dear Loraine,

We are sitting here watching our blizzard as it is beginning.
Thank goodness for a house to be in. We want to thank
you for all your hospitality over the years and all the
support you have given our family, coming to our kids'
grad parties and showers, etc.

We're glad you have a wonderful family caring for you now
as you have cared for everyone over the years.

Much love,

Howie & Char & families

Laverne Ronkainen | April 11, 2008

Hi,

What a blustery day! The TV has even been blown off the air. First channels 6 & 8 went and now even 10 is off the air. There was a 62-mph wind gust at the airport. I don't believe we got nearly the amount of snow predicted, but with the wind, it is "whiteout" conditions, and they ask us all to stay home. Remember the days when it was such "fun" to go out in the storm and see how deep a drift we could drive through?

It is great to have "memories" and we will always remember all the times we were together...the good and the bad. The good...when we had our kids and all the fun times and the bad...when we lost Herman, Mom, Dad, Carol and Vi.

We hope your day goes well and that you can enjoy some more dialogues with Jacob!

Love, Laverne

White as Snow

April 11, 2008 - 1:47 p.m.

When we have snow, I am always reminded of God's grace. *"Though your sins are like scarlet, they shall be as white as snow"* (Isaiah 1:18).

Schools were canceled here (even ours). Since Mom has been staying in bed, I raised her bed yesterday afternoon so she could see the snow blowing around. She raised the bed herself this morning so she could continue to look at the blustery weather. She said she felt better this morning—not so gasping for breath—however, that was before she sat up and moved a little bit. Her appetite was a little better yesterday, and so far, it is even better today. I am enjoying these last days to talk, reminisce and sing with my mom. I will always treasure these days as a gift from God.

My sister is coming tomorrow, and we hope to finish cleaning out Mom's apartment. I even ran there this morning to empty a few things. Yesterday, Jim, Sarah and I ran to the apartment to pack some more boxes and left Rachel with Grandma duties. Mom nearly died laughing when Rachel walked in with a chip clip on her nose to empty the commode. Mom wished she'd had her camera. There is no shortage of laughter for Mom with the grandkids around.

Thanks to Cherie and Theresa for dinner tonight and last night so I didn't have to take the energy to think about what to feed my family. Mom also enjoyed a visit from Cherie and Doris today. Thanks for all your calls, prayers, and words of encouragement for me as well as

my mom. It means so much to me. To God alone be the glory.

Mom's apartment was about a block away from our house, close enough so that if I stood at the park near our house and she stood at the parking lot entrance to her apartment building, we could watch the kids walk to her place. I remember when she was selling her house in Esko, Minnesota, the house I grew up in, she told my Aunt Laverne, "I have to go down and help Kay with those kids." Through the years, I had asked her if she ever regretted the decision. She always adamantly responded, "No." She never regretted all the time she spent with her grandchildren. She adored them, and they adored her.

~~~

The Grandchildren

L to R: Jacob, Jimmy, Alexander, Sarah, & Rachel

Todd Wuollet | April 11, 2008

Hi, Auntie

The house on Ridge Road meant many things to me as a child...
There were many games of Scrabble, Clue and Trivial Pursuit played on the kitchen table. Part of the way through any game, there would be a plethora of bars and cookies presented to the table on a tiered serving dish. Juice was the beverage of choice until we acquired a taste for coffee, and others graduated to hot chocolate. Mary and Kay were formidable opponents in any game. They were also the daughters of a teacher, and being proud of their accomplishments, they would explain in detail of how they won. My brothers and I became very formidable opponents as well. We always had fun and the house was filled with laughter, harmonized by the baked goodies, juice and generosity.
I love you Auntie,
Todd

The House on Ridge Road

Heather Bergstedt | April 11, 2008 - 12:13 p.m.

Greetings from the blustery north!

Loraine, we always think of you after blizzards such as the one we are in the midst of right now. Brian has never felt the need for a snow blower since he continues, to this day, to clear our driveway with your old snow scoop! Unfortunately, it will be in much use after this storm passes.

I can't help but liken your current trials to a raging blizzard. The winds howl and snow temporarily obstructs our view, but we have the hope of spring to come. Soon the daffodils and tulips will bloom. We pray that you find peace and comfort in the midst of the storm and hold in your heart the hope of eternal spring.

We pray that the love of Christ will continue to surround you and your loved ones. We love you all.

Brian and Heather

Karen Gudim | April 11, 2008

Loraine,

I want to thank you for the special "doll" memories my girls, Lori and Janelle, have from your apartment. They loved being there! They each treasure their "breakable dolls" that came from Rachel after our fire.

Thanks for your love and kindness.

98

Too Much Stuff

April 12, 2008 - 7:43 p.m.

"Yet I am always with you; you hold me by my right hand. You guide me with your counsel, and afterward you will take me into glory. Whom have I in heaven but you? And earth has nothing I desire besides you. My flesh and my heart may fail, but God is the strength of my heart and my portion forever" (Psalm 73:23-26).

Mom is sleeping now. This evening was the first time she asked for the air hunger meds, so I know she was having a hard time getting her breath. She is sleeping now, which is a little early for her, but the meds will do that. Our friend, Carol, helped my sister and me finish cleaning Mom's apartment. Elaine, Dick and Jim and then Todd visited Mom this afternoon.

Mom is looking forward to the day she will be taken into glory. We are praying that for her sake it will be soon. S.D.G.

Every time I came back from clearing out Mom's apartment, she would say, "Too much stuff. People collect too much stuff, and we can't take it with us when we die." She had already downsized when she moved from Esko. Now she instructed us to give all her stuff away. What the grandkids didn't want, she wanted it to go to her nieces and nephews or other friends and relatives who were just starting out and furnishing their own places. What didn't go, she wanted donated to the library book sale and Finn Fest fundraiser. That was Mom—so giving.

April 13, 2008 - 6:42 p.m.

Hi Loraine,

Thought I would reminisce a little... the Lakers Basketball Game you took me to in 1948 was one of the highlights of my childhood. You, Laverne and Vi were always there for me and my kids when the chips were down. Thank you for being a great sister during my times of woe. I hope I can be as strong as you when it's my time to meet my Maker.

God's Peace and Love Always,

Clyde and Lou Ann

April 13, 2008 - 8:29 p.m.

"I love you, O Lord, my strength" (Psalm 18:1 NASB).

Praise the Lord! I could not do this without His strength.

Thanks, Carol and Ardella for brightening my mom's day with your visit. She was feeling a little down today. We were humored this weekend by a letter from the county requiring Mom for jury duty. All those years we lived in Esko, she was never called, and now, twice in the last ten years, she is summoned here. We did send it back with her regrets.

Someone at the courthouse actually called Mom back to tell her she couldn't decline. This individual must not have looked at Mom's birthdate. Mom said, "I most certainly can decline. I'm 80 years old and dying of cancer." You go, girl! Confrontation was apparently easier on the phone.

Mom's breathing seemed a little better today. She only had her air hunger meds three times today. Her appetite was better as well. However, if you want to lose weight, the Loraine diet would work well. :) She eats toddler portions, maybe even less than that. Please pray that she would not become depressed over her illness. She has been a real trooper about all of this. She does not complain about anything. What an example she is to me. S.D.G.

April 14, 2008 - 1:16 p.m.

Psalm 84 is one of my favorite Psalms. Verse 12 says, *"O Lord Almighty, blessed is the man who trusts in you."*

Both Mom and I are blessed because we trust in Him. We are looking forward to eternity with Christ.

The nurse was here today. Mom's vitals were better today and the fluid is gone from her lungs, so she is off the Lasix, a diuretic. Praise the Lord! The nurse said she was finally stable although she is very fragile. Her condition could change in an instant. We are continuing with our plans to be gone this weekend for the homeschool conference in Duluth. My cousin, Patti, and my sister will be coming to care for Mom while we are gone. Please pray that the fluid would not build up in her lungs again.

We are praying for you Jim, Dee and your whole family. To God alone, be the glory.

Grandma Sitting Duties

April 15, 2008 - 10:42 a.m.

Grandma, you have been such a blessing in my life. I just want to say thank you for being there for me. You have taught me to be nice to others even when I don't feel like it. I appreciate you for always keeping your calm when I'm driving; it must have been tough sitting in the passenger seat!

Love, Jimmy

    Jimmy, our oldest, was a huge blessing to me in this journey. He frequently had "Grandma sitting" duties. Toward the end, I would collapse into bed about 10:00 p.m. while he would sit with Mom, comfort her, and hold her hand until 1:00 a.m. Then he'd wake me up to take the night shift. He would even remind me, "Mom, I've got this. Go to bed. I will sit with Grandma."

Mom and Jimmy

Blessed Be Your Name

April 15, 2008 - 4:37 p.m.

"I will extol You, my God, O King; and I will bless Your name forever and ever. Every day I will bless You. And I will praise Your name forever and ever" (Psalm 145:1-2 NKJV).

The song "Blessed Be Your Name"[5] by Matt Redman has been going through my head all day. One verse in particular discusses pain and suffering in our journey.

So, can you guess the kind of day we had? By 8:45 this morning, I had already given my mom two doses of the air hunger meds. I called hospice and a nurse came out to check her and confirmed what I had heard - fluid on the right lung again. I am praying that she will not suffer and she not linger, On the other hand, I am treasuring these last days with her, and it will hurt to lose her. As it says in Job 1:21b (ESV): *"The Lord gave, and the Lord has taken away; blessed be the name of the Lord."*

April 16, 2008 - 2:54 p.m.

Dear Kay and family –

God gives us courage and strength for each day, and He will take care of us until our time comes to go home to Heaven. Greet your mom for me with a big hug. Our thoughts and prayers are with you all.

God's peace and love,

Deanna and Jerry

April 16, 2008 - 9:55 p.m.

"The Lord is good, a refuge in times of trouble" (Nahum 1:7).

Mom did not have a good day. I thought she was going to faint on me this morning. She is getting weaker by the day. Today she was also very nauseated. I had to pick up an anti-nausea med for her. Company brightened her spirit though. Yesterday, Joel, Patti, Jason, Tara, Evan and Neveah came to visit her in the afternoon and Calvin and Carolyn and my friend, Carol, in the evening. Today, Aileen came in the morning and Marty, JoAnn, and Josh came in the afternoon. JoAnn sat with Mom so I could go watch Rachel and her derby race at AWANA.

Thanks for the visits, letters, calls, prayers and e-mails. You are an encouragement to my family, my mom and to me. Soli Deo Gloria.

Ellen Friday | April 16, 2008

Dear Kay,

God bless you and your family during this precious time with your mom. I remember the special time with my mom just before she went to be with Jesus. These will be forever memories for you. It has been such a joy knowing you and your mom these years even though it has been a while since we have seen you.

I wonder, Loraine, if you remember at Patti and Joe's wedding on the boat how our moms had such a good time visiting. It was a wonderful time for mom and came just before she got really sick.

Jesus is faithful especially when the going seems really tough. Tonight, at church, we had this wonderful study in the book of Ephesians about how very much God loves and wants an intimate relationship with us, and it seems you have been leaning on that shoulder. One of my favorite verses is in Deuteronomy 33:12: *"Let the beloved of the Lord rest secure in Him for He shields him all day long and the one the Lord loves rests between His shoulders."*

I'm praying for you,

Ellen Friday

Lifeline

April 17, 2008 - 3:35 p.m.

"Therefore do not worry about tomorrow, for tomorrow will worry about itself. Each day has enough trouble of its own" (Matthew 6:34).

I'm sure I would have panicked if I'd known what today was going to be like. I woke at 4:15 a.m. to my mom retching and gasping for breath. I gave her the air hunger and her anti-nausea meds, prayed with her and sang softly to her. Her nausea seemed to be alleviated, but she was still gasping for air. I thought that this was it. I began praying "God, how can I help her?" I was prompted to check the oxygen machine. The machine read less than 1L of air, so I quickly switched her to her portable tank. It's amazing what a difference oxygen makes! (I've been comparing this event with Christ and how—with Him as our lifeline—what a difference He makes in our lives). Her color was back to normal within ten minutes.

I then called the Apria medical supply company, and the answering service faxed an order to them. I thought I had eight hours of oxygen left on the portable tanks, but that would be if she were on 2L, not 4L. In reality, she was using up the oxygen twice as fast as I thought. I realized this at 7:30 and called back at 8:00 and left another message. I called again at 8:30, and the guy in charge was a little irate that the answering service had not informed him at 5:30 a.m. before it was a crisis situation. He made it here with a few minutes of oxygen to spare and showed me that part of a hose connecting the water had plugged.

Anyway, the crisis was averted, and we got on with our day. We can laugh about it now. I'm thankful that it happened early this morning and not tonight since my cousin, Patti, will be staying with my mom. My sister is coming tomorrow afternoon. Thanks to Marty, JoAnn and Josh for staying until the guy came. They were ready to run up to St. Cloud to get the oxygen. LaVerne Rengo, Jeannette H, and Jeannette R. came to visit, too. Mom looked pretty good for all she had been through.

The nurse came by, and because we are switching meds due to the nausea, she will be coming everyday through the weekend. Mom's vitals were a bit off too. Her blood pressure was 102/60, pulse was up to 112 and oxygen was 86 percent. She did feel well enough to have her coffee today though, so that is a good thing. I'll be gone for the weekend, so I will not be updating the site until Sunday. To God alone be the glory—forever.

April 19, 2008 - 1:23 p.m.

Dear Grandma,

Thank you for letting us sleep over at your house all the time. And thank you for being there for me. I am glad you are my grandma. I love you.

Love,

Rachel

Mom and Rachel

Two Machines

April 20, 2008 - 9:33 p.m.

"Praise be to the God and Father of our Lord Jesus Christ! In his great mercy he has given us new birth into a living hope through the resurrection of Jesus Christ from the dead, and into an inheritance that can never perish, spoil or fade. This inheritance is kept in heaven for you, who through faith are shielded by God's power until the coming of the salvation that is ready to be revealed in the last time. In all this you greatly rejoice, though now for a little while you may have had to suffer grief in all kinds of trials. These have come so that the proven genuineness of your faith— of greater worth than gold, which perishes even though refined by fire—may result in praise, glory and honor when Jesus Christ is revealed" (1 Peter 1:3-7).

Mom had a good weekend with Mary and Patti. She no longer needs her anti-nausea meds because the switch in the air hunger meds has eliminated her nausea. She even made it out to sit in the living room on Saturday and Sunday. We do, however, have two oxygen machines for her now and she has one running at 4L and the other at 3L for a total of 7L. I need to ask more questions about this tomorrow as my understanding is that more than 5L can damage her cells. However, lack of oxygen can cause cells to die, and her oxygen level was only at 86 percent with 5L of oxygen.

~~~~

Gail Peil | April 21, 2008

Hello Loraine, Kay, Mary and families: Just wanted to send my written thoughts your way. I have been praying that you are pain free. I will also add ease of breathing. I, too, have fond memories of your house in Esko.

Please know that my thoughts and prayers have been with you all since Kay's original email and continue to each day.

With lots of love from Cloquet—Gail

April 21, 2008 - 3:20 p.m.

"He who dwells in the shelter of the Most High will rest in the shadow of the Almighty" (Psalm 91:1).

Mom has not gotten out of bed today. She was a little more tired than the past few days. She does have fluid on both lungs again, so she is back on Lasix. (She did not have fluid on Saturday, so she had no Lasix on Sunday.) Vitals were good: BP was 122/70, oxygen was 91 percent, and her pulse was eighty-four. I asked about the oxygen levels and was told because Mom does not have chronic lung disease and will not be on oxygen for years, she can be at 7L. Controlling the air hunger so we can keep her as comfortable as possible is the goal. I asked her if the company was too much, but she said no—besides she thrives on visitors. They energize her. I teased her that maybe I should leave more often so she can have more good weekends. :) To God alone be the glory.

~~~~

April 22, 2008 - 9:09 p.m.

Dear Grandma,

I love you, and I love the sleep-overs that you let us have. I like that you read to me. I love that you let me come to your home and play with the toys you got for me.

Love,

Jacob

Mom and Jacob

Different Gifts

April 22, 2008 - 7:29 p.m.

Several verses have been running through my head today. One was Romans 12:6a: *"We have different gifts ... "* I know God was not talking about nursing, but bear with me as I am making a correlation here. I exhibited my lack of the gift of "nursing" to my mom today. She needed some nasal saline. Simple enough, or so I thought. One squirt in each nostril to relieve nasal congestion. Poor Mom got so much with my first squirt that I think she got more wet with that than her bed bath. My mom is so kind; she only said that maybe she should sit up more. Last evening, she did suggest that maybe I should go get Rachel to wheel her out to the living room since I had hit both sides of her bedroom doorway.

The other verse is John 10:14: *"I know my sheep and my sheep know me."* Humor me some as I substitute the word pharmacist for the word sheep. Today, I walked into the pharmacy, and the pharmacist said, "Yes, it came in today." I'm not sure I like being such a familiar face to the pharmacist. Seriously though, I sure am glad I know Jesus. I am hoping that you all know Jesus, and that He knows you, too.

Other than the nasal congestion, the major change that I see in my mom is that she is sleeping more. She does not usually get up at night, and she wakes up very briefly for morning meds about 7:00 a.m. and falls back to sleep for another hour and a half or so. She has got to be the most easy-going and "patient" patient I know. Bless her heart. Mary came today, and then Wanda came for a visit, so I took the time to do some necessary shopping. Thanks for all your prayers and support. S.D.G.

Harold and Martha Hanson | April 23, 2008

Hi Loraine, Kay, Mary, and all your families,

It has been a long time since we last visited. I was really stunned to hear about this huge, sudden change in your lives! I just talked to Elaine Sunday night, and she filled me in after their visit on last Saturday. I have also filled in my kids, Jonas, Nathan and Lisa. They all remember you very well from all those years in Esko and visiting at Mom and Dad's house, church, and at Loraine's. (Nathan remembered Loraine as "Grandma's jogging partner" from all the long walks they would take.) We are all thinking about you and doing a lot of remembering all the fun and support through a lot of events.

Jumalan Rauhaan,

Martha

April 23, 2008 - 8:48 p.m.

"The length of our days is seventy years—or eighty, if we have the strength..." (Psalm 90:10).

I thought this verse appropriate for my mom. She is one strong lady. She joined us in the living room today, and right away, Jacob crawled up next to her and asked her to read. She read him one whole book and then part of another before she had to stop. She was also amused as she listened to her grandchildren getting grossed out while they were dissecting an earthworm for science class today.

Mom's blood pressure was low today, 90/42, so the nurse is going to keep an eye on it to see if her body is starting to shut down or if the low reading has anything to do with the Lasix and dehydration. Her oxygen was still hanging around 90 percent and she still has fluid on her lower lungs.

Guy and Geneva Howe came to visit her tonight. They are the managers at her apartment building. We finished moving the last of the furniture out this afternoon and evening, so thanks to Chris, Kristin and family for the Subway gift card. The timing was great, and we enjoyed the meal tonight. Thanks also for your prayers and support. S.D.G.

Donna Kovala | April 24, 2008

Dear Loraine and Kay,

Jumalan Terve! (God's greetings)

I think of you every day and wonder how everything is going. We all are on that road Home, some sooner and some later. It is a comfort that our sins are forgiven in Jesus Christ, and in His grace, we will reach Heaven.

Praises to God!

~~~~

April 24, 2008 - 9:54 p.m.

"I will bless the Lord at all times: His praise shall continually be in my mouth. My soul shall make its boast in the Lord: The humble shall hear of it and be glad. Oh, magnify the Lord with me, And let us exalt His name together. I sought the Lord, and He heard me. And delivered me from all my fears" (Psalm 34:1-4 NKJV).

It has been a busy day. Loraine has had a lot of company: Laverne, Jerry, Tim, Patti, Clyde, Calvin, and Carolyn (hope I didn't miss anyone). Loraine was able to sit in the living room to visit for a while. Thanks to all those who stopped by to visit.

Kay is taking a break from the Journal today. She had worship practice tonight and is spending some quality time with our little ones.

Thanks to all for your thoughts and prayers!

In Christ, Chuck

Deanna Kivi | April 24, 2008

Dear Kay,

How great that your mom can be surrounded by family.
Loraine, you are such a "patient" patient as Kay describes
you, and that's the person you are—caring and
appreciative of others. God surely does give us courage
and strength as we travel this life. We are thinking of you.

In God's peace and grace,

Love, Jerry and Deanna

Weaker Voice

April 25, 2008 - 8:42 p.m.

"For everyone born of God overcomes the world. This is the victory that has overcome the world, even our faith. Who is it that overcomes the world? Only he who believes that Jesus is the Son of God" (1 John 5:4-5).

I'm thankful that my mom believes that Jesus is God's Son. Though her journey on this earth is nearly over, she will soon continue her journey with Christ. Her body will die, but her spirit will live with Christ forever. Praise the Lord!

The nurse came today and Mom's vitals were within normal range, except her oxygen levels fluctuated between 88 percent & 91 percent. Jimmy noticed and commented that her voice is getting weaker. Mom said that it takes so much energy to eat and even talk. She did, however, get up this evening to join our movie night. I asked her if she thought it was rude for me to say that she didn't look very well tonight. She chuckled at that.

My cousin, Scott, stopped by for a visit as did my Uncle Ed and Aunt Joan. I think they cheered her up on a day Mom would describe as "gloomy." Thanks to Priscilla for the delicious maple syrup. We all enjoyed it with our French toast this morning. To God be the glory.

Priscilla Harvala | April 25, 2008

Dear Loraine,

God's Greetings!

My thoughts and prayers are with you every day. A bit ago, I was singing this song, and all my thoughts were of you:

"Oh beloved friends, remember, Faith in Jesus e'er to keep. For the good and loyal Shepherd, Gave His life to save His sheep: In His triumph is our strength, In His blood our nourishment. In His sacred wounds we find, Endless year of grace divine. Mercy's power will sustain us, Till in Heaven we arrive."

God's Peace!

April 26, 2008 - 7:23 p.m.

"Lord, you have been our dwelling place throughout all generations" (Psalm 90:1).

Without God as my dwelling place, this endeavor would be very difficult. Praise Him for the strength He gives me daily.

After a rough evening and night coughing, Mom's cough seems to be under control. I was concerned enough to call the nurse and have her come check Mom out to make sure there was not more fluid in the lungs. Her lungs had no more fluid, only what was there before. Her oxygen level was at 89 percent, and for some reason, the nurse could not get a blood pressure on my mom.

I joked with Mom, "Well, we know you're not dead, so there must be some other reason."

Mom has been sleeping more, so visits are for shorter times. My sister, Mary, and her family were here for a time.

Mom has been sleeping well at night; however, I am not. I am so in tune to her cough that when I heard her cough at 4:00 a.m., I got her meds and went into her room and found her sound asleep. Needless to say, I did not wake her up, but I was still awake at 5:30 when she did wake up. So, if you would please pray for me to hear her when it is only necessary. Thanks for all your prayers and support. To God be the glory.

~~~~

Alexander Criswell | April 26, 2008 - 3:13 pm

Hi Grandma!

This is Alexander. I really had fun with you as a grandma. I enjoyed the garage sales, the birthday shopping, the sleepovers, and just having you as a grandma.

Love,
Alexander

Mom and Alexander

So Grateful

April 27, 2008 - 10:14 p.m.

"The Lord himself goes before you and will be with you; he will never leave you nor forsake you. Do not be afraid; do not be discouraged" (Deuteronomy 31:8).

Loraine had a good day today. Jimmy and Sarah stayed with her this morning during our church service. Sarah and I stayed with her while the rest of the family went to a benefit for a friend suffering from amyotrophic lateral sclerosis (ALS). She sat in the living room for much of the day. She was able to watch a movie with the children, listen to our devotions, and sing with Kay, Jimmy, and Rachel before bed. Thank you for all your prayers!

In Christ,

Chuck

I am blessed to have my wonderful husband who will tell me to go rest and see that I am caring for myself as well as for my mom. It has been a stressful time for him since the headquarters for his work moved to Maple Grove, extending his commute an extra twenty miles. He has had to adjust the time he leaves for work so he doesn't get stuck in traffic. With all this, he never complains, but just helps me however he can. I am truly blessed.

LaVerne Rengo | April 28, 2008

Dear Loraine,

Jumalan Terve!

It was nice to hear you were "attending school" with your grandchildren. We certainly enjoyed our visit with you, as well as with Kay, Jim, Sarah, Rachel and Jacob. What a nice family! And we got to see the kids again in Duluth.
Our caring thoughts are with all of you again today!

In God's Peace,

LaVerne & Jim

Mottled Feet

April 28, 2008 - 3:56 p.m.

"Because of the Lord's great love, we are not consumed, for his compassions never fail. They are new every morning; great is your faithfulness" (Lamentations 3:22-23).

Praise the Lord! And thanks to all my prayer warriors. Mom only got up once at 3:30 a.m. for her air hunger meds, and I was back to sleep about 4:00. She is requiring her meds every five hours like clockwork now. Today was a good day for her as well. She has been up in the living room participating in our school day since about 11:00 a.m. The nurse came today, and Mom's oxygen was up to 94 percent. She has not had that level since she has been sick. Her BP was normal and pulse was 89, which is a little low for her, but good considering the disease. Her feet, however, were very mottled when she had them down. They were so purple, they almost looked black. Rachel told the nurse that we put her socks on because they looked so bad. We had asked her several times if she wanted them up, but she wanted to read the *Pine Journal* sitting up with her feet on the floor. Finally, she wanted them up, and the color returned to normal.

She commented to the nurse that her grandchildren keep her young. Last night, she was reminiscing after devotions about who Sarah thought the Bible applied to. When Sarah was little, she told us that the Bible only applied to men because after we pray we say, "Amen." We had a good laugh since Sarah did not even remember saying it.

Unless Mom's condition changes, I'll probably update the journal on Wednesday after the nurse comes for a visit. Thank you to all for your prayers and support. To God be the glory!

~~~~

Eric and Beth Nuutinen | April 30, 2008

Dear Loraine,

I have been thinking about you and the memories our families have shared. I bet you guys remember where you were when I house-sat in the summer of 1986. Europe? Still can remember your Esko house like it was yesterday. Hope you can stay comfortable with your meds and also in the mindset that so many people have come to love you here on earth!

God's grace and mercy are with you all.

God' peace and love,

Beth, Eric, August, George and Hilda Nuutinen

~~~~

Someday Soon

April 30, 2008 - 1:22 p.m.

"For I am convinced that neither death nor life, neither angels nor demons, neither the present nor the future, nor any powers, neither height nor depth, nor anything else in all creation, will be able to separate us from the love of God that is in Christ Jesus our Lord" (Romans 8:38-39).

Someday soon my mom will know that love, be face-to-face with God. How soon? Only God knows, but the signs are getting closer.

The nurse was here today, and Mom's oxygen level was low, so we bumped her up to 8L. She was then fluctuating between 88 to 90 percent. BP was good; pulse was 98. She was very wakeful last night. I gave her meds at 3:30 am (God woke me up just like I had asked him to). She said she was awake at 1:30 feeling like she had slept all night. She turned on her light after her meds, read and was still awake at 7:30 this morning. She has not had a morning nap and is now sitting up visiting with Bernette Sieg in the living room. You would never guess her air hunger meds are supposed to make her drowsy. Her feet, when down, were again very dark purple, and she is needing her air hunger meds more frequently during the day. The nurse will come again on Friday, unless things should deteriorate faster than expected, and as the nurse said, "Things could change in an hour." All in all, Mom's spirits are good, and she enjoyed a "concert" from Sarah, Rachel and Jacob today, complete with drums, recorder and saxophone. I'll update the site on Friday unless things change.

To God alone be the glory.

Joanne Harvala | May 1, 2008

Good day to you, Loraine!

Hopefully you're breathing is easier today—or at least more comfortable.
I remember all of our visits to your house growing up—you being a great friend to my mom, the days you spent as our substitute teacher—I was so proud to know you. You were always so nice to the students.... even when they tried to run all over "The Sub"!

May God comfort you and give you and Kay restful peace through the night.

~~~

Elaine Kumpula | May 1, 2008

Dear Loraine, Kay, Chuck, Mary, Robert and children,

We are thinking of you every day. I read the updates from Kay, et al. (yes, that is you, Chuck) each morning before I even think of looking at anything else.

Loraine, you were Mom's special friend and neighbor for so many years. How much better can it get? We are blessed.

God's Peace and love you all,

Elaine, Dick and boys

134

Imminent Signs

May 1, 2008 - 12:45 a.m.

"As for me, I know that my Redeemer lives, And at the last He will take His stand on the earth. Even after my skin is destroyed, Yet from my flesh I shall see God; Who I myself shall behold, And whom my eyes shall see and not another" (Job 19:25-27 NASB).

The nurse was here today and thought Mom might pass away this weekend. She is showing imminent signs of death. She has been needing her air hunger meds every one to two hours, and I've been giving another med to help her breathing every four hours. She has been sleeping most of the day, and her labored breathing stops for about ten seconds and then will start up again for a while.

She was able to visit Jodie, Becky and the kids today, and Wanda, Bill, Bobby, Ida and Mary this evening. My sister, Mary, is staying with her tonight along with Alexander (her son) and Jimmy. I will update you as needed tomorrow. Please continue to pray that she be kept comfortable until she goes to be with the Lord. To God alone be the glory.

Paula Thrall | May 1, 2008

Dear Loraine,

Growing up I spent so much time at your house, but there is one memory that I am reminded of when the weather goes below zero. I have this distinct memory of being at your house during a snowstorm. Big snow drifts and record-busting wind-chill of 150 degrees below... maybe more. I must have been twelve... I don't remember. We were trying to decide whether someone, I think Herman, should drive me home or not. It's all very fuzzy. But, to this day, when the weather gets really cold, and the weathermen start talking about how bad it's going to get, I remember that day. I just think back to that time and kind of chuckle. Somehow, we lived through all that... without four-wheel drives, Gore-Tex, cellphones and Internet. We just figured it out. And you too, somehow, after Herman passed, figured it all out with two girls to boot. As I think about it, perhaps you were one of my 'town-mom' role models...

Your home and yard was always tidy. Your kitchen was small, but it packed the punch. Your fridge had the best snacks in town. You even had POP. We got to play music and records. In fact, when I hear Abba on the oldies radio station, I think of Kay and I sneaking Mary's records. We played games at your kitchen table for hours on end, too. Kay always won. She was a tough competitor. Golly, I wonder where she got that from? To set the record straight, I still can't shuffle a deck and couldn't tell you the rules for Rummy, Rook, much less Crazy 8's, even if my life depended on it.

Thank you, dear Loraine, for taking me in and opening your heart and home over the years. I've learned so much from your strength and caring... what it means to be a strong mother with a tender heart.

May the peace, love and comfort of God be with you (and Kay, Mary and their families too) in these final days 'til you are resting finally at Home with Him above...

Love, Paula

May 1, 2008 - 7:44 p.m.

"And I heard a voice from heaven saying, 'Write this down: Blessed are those who die in the Lord from now on. Yes, says the Spirit, they are blessed indeed, for they will rest from all their toils and trials, for their good deeds follow them!'" (Revelation 14:13 NLT).

Loraine has had a more difficult day breathing. She is now taking her air hunger medicine more frequently—every two to three hours.

Loraine was able to sit in the living room for supper tonight. She was eagerly awaiting Jimmy from his "shop" adventure with our neighbor known as "Mr. Bill." Jimmy was helping him put a swing set together in a suburb of the Twin Cities.

Kay and her friend, Carol, are singing old hymns along with Loraine tonight.

We appreciate your prayers and notes!

In Christ,

Chuck

The Annuity

May 2nd was not only my husband's birthday, but also the day Mom's annuity came due, so she requested that I leave immediately when the bank opened to cash it out. Even though I had told her that at her death it would come due anyway, she wanted me to cash it out so she could pay for her funeral. It was one last thing she could check off her list. (I wonder if that is why she is hanging on so long). Anyway, since it was Chuck's birthday, I asked my sister to stay with Mom, and we rented a room at the local hotel. It was the first full night's sleep I'd had since the middle of April when we went to the Minnesota Association of Christian Home Educators (MACHE) conference. Though we ended up with a room on the side near the train tracks, I slept so soundly that I never heard a thing. God refreshed me abundantly.

May 2, 2008 - 10:06 p.m.

"As for me, I know that my Redeemer lives, And at the last He will take His stand on the earth. Even after my skin is destroyed, yet from my flesh I shall see God; Whom I myself shall behold, And whom my eyes shall see and not another..." (Job 19:25-27 NASB).

I'm having trouble accessing the site from a different computer so I had to go through the guest book. Mom is showing imminent signs of death, so I will update you more tomorrow from home. My sister, Mary, is staying with Mom tonight as are Alexander and Jimmy. Please continue to pray that she will be kept comfortable until the time she goes to be with the Lord. S.D.G.

~~~~

Gretchyn Quernemoen | May 2, 2008

Kay, I am praying for you and your family today! You are such a true inspiration as you look to God for your strength and comfort! Keep strong in Him!

~~~~

Laverne Ronkainen | May 2, 2008
Hi Loraine,

Just a final farewell from us. We love you and will see you again someday when we will all have new bodies...no pain, sorrow or crying... when we meet on that heavenly shore.

I'm baking cinnamon rolls and would love to have you over for coffee and a good chat. Take care and God Bless you!

Thanks, Kay, for all your updates. You have been a real blessing to all of us who read your messages and especially to your mom.

Love, Jerry and Laverne

~~~~

Lou Ann Rengo | May 2, 2008

Hi Loraine,

Just a short note to say we love you and you will be rejoicing with the Lord soon.

Love,

Lou Ann

God Awakens Mary

May 3, 2008 - 11:23 a.m.

"And the dead man came out, his hands and feet wrapped with strips of linen, and a cloth around his face" (John 11:44).

Now I have a clearer understanding of what Kay has been doing. After suddenly waking to a couple of strange noises, I heard a loud CLUNK at 1:00 a.m.

I rushed into Mom's room and found Mom slumped to the side of her bed, her arm bent strangely underneath her and her head pressing on the bed rail. I was sure she had died. "Mom?" I asked. As I was reaching for her, I heard a magnificent snore. She was so sound asleep she hadn't even felt herself bump her head.

After I rearranged her on her pillow, I went back to bed, but had too much adrenaline to sleep. I ended up staying awake until her next meds were due at 3:15. Then, exhausted, I fell sound asleep.

I just as immediately awoke at 7:15 with an urgent message flashing through my head: MEDICATION. I was thankful that Kay had told me to pray that God would awaken me when needed.

Mom actually asked for breakfast this morning, and her color is a little better, but still gray. Chuck and Kay stopped at home to see her, and Chuck said that I was a miracle worker because every time I come up to stay with her, she gets better.

The real story is that Kay discovers problems with the oxygen equipment, goes through all the terror of Mom not being able to breathe, calls the equipment technicians, and arranges for and takes delivery of a new machine. I arrive about a half hour after the chaos subsides and get credit for Mom's improvement.

The nurse has arranged daily visits now with the expectation that Mom has very little time left probably more so than was thought yesterday, but only God knows how long.

Mary

Renee Pouchak | May 3, 2008

Proverbs 18:10: *"The Name of the Lord is a strong tower; the righteous run to it and are safe."*

Praise God you are always in His capable Hands. Our prayers are for strength and comfort for all of you, dear Loraine, and our dear friends, Chuck and Kay and family. I believe that you are really experiencing the sweet presence of God through this as He promises. May you even have a fuller measure of Him!

~~~~

Lisa Sell | May 3, 2008

Kay, Mary, and families,

You are in my thoughts as you and your mom continue your journey.

~~~~

Heidi Brings | May 3, 2008 - 1:20 a.m.

Loraine, Kay, Mary, and families,

Our prayers and thoughts will be with you throughout this weekend, as they have been in these past couple of months. It was wonderful seeing you, Loraine, surrounded by the comfort and love of your family a few weekends ago. Kai and I were very happy that you were able to meet our family and see our kids. They all enjoyed the day at your home and have been keeping you in their special prayers since we were there.
I wish you God's speed and mercy as you go forward in your journey to heaven. Your love for God is magnified by the love and Christian values of your family at this time. It has been a real blessing for me to have known you throughout the years. Thank goodness for your wonderful sister and family for keeping that big German around enough to want to keep on coming back to Minnesota! Already looking forward to the day that we meet again...

Our love and prayers to you all.

Heidi and Kai Brings and family

148

Goodbyes Begin

May 4, 2008 - 2:50 p.m.

"...and God will wipe every tear from their eyes"
(Revelation 7:17).

Just one of those days. I look forward to the day when I'm in heaven, and there will be no more tears.

Alexander said good bye and he, my mom, and Jimmy ended up in tears because Mom thought it would be the last time she would see him.

When Mom is awake enough to talk, she can barely whisper. I tried to sing to her this afternoon but choked up and could not continue, so I found the *a cappella* tape of hymns Mom had grown up with that I had made about twelve years ago. Now she has that playing in her room.

The nurse was here and her stats were down from yesterday. Mom is not in any pain, but this is the first day that she admitted to feeling rotten.

Patti was here to watch her this morning and was shocked at the change from Thursday.

We would like to thank all the people who have come to visit Mom, and those who have helped us out in so many ways. To God be the glory.

Kay

Soft and Tender Goodbye

May 5, 2008 - 5:56 p.m.

"I will lift up my eyes to the mountains; From where shall my help come? My help comes from the Lord Who made heaven and earth. He will not allow your foot to slip; He who keeps you will not slumber" (Psalm 121:1-3 NASB).

Mom (actually all of us) had a tearful day yesterday. Yesterday afternoon, my cousin, Todd, visited and told my mom he had written a song for her. He had not even sung the words, and she was crying. The song was a beautiful tribute.

My cousin, Todd, played his guitar and sang the song he'd written, "Soft and Tender Goodbye," for Mom.

"Soft and Tender Goodbye"[6] by Todd Wuollet

1. *My life's been filled with blessings,*
from all the people that I've known
From all their wisdom and thoughtful caring ways
Through all the tears and laughter
and hard lessons I've had to learn
I'm so glad they were there to help me through.

Chorus:

To share in all the joy and happiness
and a shoulder to cry on when times were hard
A hardy greeting of hello,
a visit filled with love and fellowship
Followed by a soft and tender goodbye

2. When I was growing up
I thought I could do it on my own
I soon found out that I was wrong.
But you were an example of a faith as strong as stone,
You showed me there's always someone with arms open
wide.

(Chorus)

3. When time becomes short,
every day is a precious gift
ordinary things are no longer common place.
Memories of old times,
embarrassing moments cause us to laugh
A quiet smile expressing more than words can say.

(Chorus)

Mom's brother, Clyde, along with his wife, Lou Ann, came a bit later, saw Mom crying, and joined us in our river of pain. We sang her favorite hymns to Mom for quite some time and were rewarded by the peaceful smile that soon shined on her face.

My sister came up for the night, and Mom asked her where our dad was. Mom started sobbing when Mary replied that he was in heaven waiting for her. She then asked for me and told me that she thought that my dad would be there for her. I again told her that Dad was waiting in heaven for her.

Mom did not want to be alone last night and was very anxious. Mary and our friend, Wanda, took turns sitting with her every two hours through the night so I could rest.

Today, Mom was less anxious. The nurse was here, and Mom's stats were down even more than yesterday. She is no longer able to eat or drink. We have been giving her water when she asks (which is not often) by means of a syringe.

Mom's brother, Calvin, and niece, Carolyn, just came to visit. Even now I can hear them singing hymns to her. Thank you for all your prayers. Please continue to lift us up in prayer as we continue to lift our eyes to our Lord from whence our help comes.

To God alone be the glory.

Teri Zub | May 5, 2008 - 6:53 p.m.

Hello Auntie Loraine,

I just wanted to let you know that you and your family continue to be in our prayers. Thank you for always being there for us. We are blessed to have such a SWEET & CARING Auntie. We love you very much!

Teri

Final Farewells

May 6, 2008 - 9:20 p.m.

"For we know that when this earthly tent we live in is taken down—when we die and leave these bodies—we will have a home in heaven, an eternal body made for us by God himself and not by human hands. We grow weary in our present bodies, and we long for the day when we will put on our heavenly bodies like new clothing. For we will not be spirits without bodies, but we will put on new heavenly bodies. Our dying bodies will be swallowed up by everlasting life. God himself has prepared us for this, and a guarantee he has given us his Holy Spirit. So we are always confident, even though we know that as long as we live in these bodies we are not at home with the Lord. That is why we live by believing and not by seeing. Yes, we are fully confident, and we would rather be away from these bodies, for then we will be at home with the Lord" (2 Corinthians 5:1-8 NLT).

Loraine's body continues to deteriorate. She can only answer yes or no and needs to take water from a dropper. Kay and Wanda took shifts last night to lie next to Loraine and hold her hand during the night for her comfort. Mary came back this morning and spent time with her until this afternoon. Carol stopped by this evening to spend time with Loraine also. Jerry, Laverne, and Tim came down from Cloquet tonight to say their final farewells and to sing hymns to her.

It's been hard to see her body deteriorate so quickly; however, we know that soon she will be with Jesus, praising our Lord in heaven with her new body.

Thanks to all for your continued prayers and support.

In Christ,

Chuck

~~~

Earlier in the day, I had talked with Tammy (my cousin, David's wife, and my friend) and mentioned Mom seemed to be lingering. She wondered if my mom needed to say one final goodbye to her sister, Laverne. Next thing I knew, Auntie Laverne, Uncle Jerry, and their grandson Tim were coming down. I'm sure the two and one-fourth hour drive was accomplished in under two hours with Auntie's driving. They arrived about 9:00 p.m. Laverne and Jerry sat by Mom's bed and sang to her, and Laverne told Mom that she could go. My sister and I had already told Mom several times that she could go. I had to walk out of the room when Auntie sang, "God Be with You 'Til We Meet Again," to my mom.

~~~

The Last Day

Wednesday, May 7, 2008

Mom spent a restless night requiring air hunger meds every half hour. I slept by her side in the recliner talking to her, giving her meds and holding her hand. Have you ever held an old person's hand? I love the touch of old people's hands. Anyway, Wanda had offered to stay, but I had sent her home for the night. I ended up calling her just before 6:30 in the morning to relieve me.

After collapsing into bed, I cried to God, "I can't do this anymore. I know it's by Your strength, but I just can't do it anymore." Sleep claimed me then. Startled awake at 8:30 a.m. by the phone, Mom's nurse, Lesa, informed me she would come in the afternoon.

"Well, I hope she lives that long," I replied. A long pause followed.

"Let me see what I can do," Lesa replied after I explained what the night had been like. Ten minutes later, she called back and said she would be there as soon as possible. Lesa arrived at 9:30 a.m. and instructed us to give the meds alternating every half hour. Mom's blood pressure on the top was seventy-two. The bottom number wasn't even registering. Death was imminent.

I called my sister, and she arrived in early afternoon. Uncle Calvin came that afternoon and knew Mom wouldn't live much longer. The hospice night nurse called to check on us about 6:30 p.m., asked how we were doing, reviewed with us what to expect, and informed us when to call her.

Later that evening on May 7 - 10:41 p.m.

"Precious in the sight of the Lord is the death of His saints" (Psalm 116:15).

Loraine passed away quietly at 9:07 pm, Wednesday, May 7th, with her daughters, Kay's family, and friends by her side. We can tell by her face that she is at peace.

Details and plans to follow tomorrow.

Thank you, all of our *Caring Bridge*® friends, for your prayers and support. We read all of the messages to Mom as they arrived, and she enjoyed hearing from you.

Mary and Kay

~~~~

Mark Lukkarila | May 8, 2008

Kay and Chuck, and family, Mary and Bob, and family;

Our deepest sympathy goes out to you all. Loraine was one of the kindest souls we have had the honor of knowing. She will be missed. We have always enjoyed the time we have spent with her.

~~~~

Not wanting to face Mother's Day on Sunday, May 11th and then Mom's funeral, we elected to have her visitation on Friday night, with the funeral on Saturday, May 10th. My cousin, David, said that Mom's visitation was a celebration of her life. That was our intent. After her funeral, she was buried next to her beloved husband. Though they had been parted by his death for almost twenty-nine years, they were once again reunited in heaven on May 7, 2008.

~~~~~

Heather Bergstedt | May 8, 2008

Kay, Mary, and Families~

We extend our deepest sympathies. Loraine was a loving, beautiful person and made the world a better place. We can rejoice that she is now at rest, breathing freely, & reunited with your dad. We rejoice for her, yet we share your grief.

"Come to Me, all you who labor and are heavy laden, and I will give you rest" Matthew 11:28.

We love you and lift you up in prayer.

Brian, Heather, Amanda, Megan & Seth

~~~~~

Strength for Every Step

May 28, 2008 - 11:07 a.m.

"Now we know that if the earthly tent we live in is destroyed, we have a building from God, an eternal house in heaven, not built by human hands. Meanwhile we groan, longing to be clothed with our heavenly dwelling ... For while we are in this tent, we groan and are burdened, because we do not wish to be unclothed but to be clothed with our heavenly dwelling, so that what is mortal may be swallowed up in life. Now it is God who has made us for this very purpose and has given us the Spirit as a deposit guaranteeing what is to come... And he (Christ) died for all, that those who live should no longer live for themselves, but for Him who died for them and was raised" (2 Corinthians 5:1-2, 4-5, 15). I loved these verses so much that I had to use them again.

It has already been three weeks since my mom went to be with our Lord. Meanwhile, those of us left here long for the day when we will be reunited with her in glory. Until that time, we are left to not only carry on but also to continue to live for Christ.

God is good—all the time. I wanted to share how faithful God is, how He worked the smallest detail, how He answered prayers, and how He strengthened me for this journey.

Every step of this journey, God faithfully provided what and who I needed to complete this journey to the end. I have mentioned them all previously. I just want to recap the last few days of my mom's life.

The last three days of my mom's life, she needed 24-hour care. We were giving her meds twenty times per day— at least every hour and on Wednesday, every half hour— to help with air hunger and anxiety. I spent early Wednesday morning (1:00 a.m. to 6:30 a.m.) sitting with my mom, singing softly to her, holding her hand, and giving her meds. My friend, Wanda, took over about 6:30 so I could sleep.

I collapsed on my bed and cried out to the Lord that I did not think I could do this anymore. This was the first time during this journey that I had felt that even with His strength, I could not do it anymore; I had no reserves left. But thankfully, God never has to run on reserves. The nurse's call, informing me that she would be here in the afternoon, woke me at 8:30 a.m. God—my Portion and my Strength—used the two hours of sleep to revive me so I could carry on throughout the day. After being apprised of my mom's condition, the nurse came at 9:30 a.m. and instructed us to give the meds alternating every half hour. Mom's blood pressure on the top was seventy-two. The bottom number wasn't even registering.

One of my prayers was that my sister, Mary, would be present when my mom died. I called Mary with an update about 10:30 a.m., and she arrived in the early afternoon. Mom's brother, Calvin, came to see her in the afternoon and knew she wouldn't live very long. Another one of my prayers was that Chuck would also be home when my mom died. He arrived home from work and took the kids to the last AWANA awards night and was back home about 8:00 p.m. When Mom continued to deteriorate, he ran to get Sarah from youth group and was also present when Mom died. I had also prayed and asked Tammy to pray that Mom's death would be in a timely manner, because even though my Aunt Laverne requested I wake her up if Mom died in the middle of the night, I was not about to wake her up then. I had also been praying that Mom's death would happen at a time when it would go unnoticed by the neighborhood. God worked out these small details much better than I could have believed. Mom's death just after 9:00 p.m. gave us the needed time to call her siblings, and she wasn't taken from here by the undertaker until after 11:00 p.m. Late enough so most people did not notice the hearse arriving at or leaving from our house.

I had consistently prayed throughout this journey that my mom's death would be peaceful. I had no idea what to expect, but it was so peaceful. God put the necessary people here to share and comfort us as Mom was dying. Wanda and Carol were here and helped us sing Mom into glory. They helped in so many ways—both during and after—and yet they thanked us for allowing them to be part of it. All the thanks go to God and how He orchestrated all the events to work out.

God provided me with unimaginable strength for this journey. The last day, it was just enough strength to do the next thing. Now it is strength to face each day without her. I miss Mom dearly. She had been an everyday part of my life and the lives of my children for the past thirteen years when she moved down to be by us. She was even more a part of our lives when she moved into our house for the last six weeks of her life. God still provides me with a peace that surpasses all understanding. He continues to guide me and satisfy my soul (see Isaiah 58:11).

We continue to grieve her loss but not as those who grieve without hope. *"For to me, to live is Christ, to die is gain"* *(Philippians 1:21).*

Thanks to all of you for your prayers, support, meals and friendship. We could not have done this without you and definitely could not have done it without God. He continues to provide for us what we need each day.

To God alone be the glory.

Kay

~~~~

Renee Pouchak | May 28, 2008

Dear Chuck, Kay, Jim, Sarah, Rachel, and Jacob,

What a lovely thing you did for your mother, mother-in-law, & grandma! We watched from the side as you lovingly cared for her at great expense to your time, independence, strength, and personal space, yet you did it with grace. It was a privilege to see her on her last Sunday and to see the family gather around holding her up and supporting each other. We have three parents between us, and we don't know our futures with them, but you have given us a beautiful role model in your family. Thank you for sharing the journey with us through your journal and all the wonderful scripture that sustains when nothing else can. *"Precious in the sight of the Lord is the death of his saints"* Psalm 116:15. We love you!

The Pouchaks

~~~~

One Year Later

May 7, 2009 - 10:29 a.m.

It is hard to believe it has been a year since my mom passed away. We have learned much through this season of grief.

I want to share some thoughts on grief and life from the kids:

"Enjoy time with the people you have left because you don't know how much time you or other people will have left." Rachel

"Grief is a process." Jimmy

"God's answer to prayer may be a yes or a no." Rachel

"Music is good therapy." Rachel, Jimmy & Jacob

"Gardening, flowers & roses are good therapy." Sarah

"It is not a good idea to go without food for many days when you are grieving—it makes you weak." Sarah

"I ate a lot more." Rachel

"It is important to spend time in God's Word even when you are mad at God. Don't use grief as an excuse to not be in God's Word — that is lame." Jimmy

"God works all things for our good." Rachel

"Grief takes a lot of energy." Sarah

"Reactions differ to grieving depending on your personality—whether you are an introvert or extrovert." Jimmy & Sarah

"You may think you have other problems, but it may only be a reaction to grief." Jimmy

"Mom needed a physical outlet for her grief, something she could control, so she spent the summer tearing apart and redoing the house. We worked all summer, and we did not need the physical outlet." Jimmy, Sarah, Rachel & Jacob

Our favorite book to help us understand grief: "Tear Soup"[7] by Pat Schweibert and Chuck DeKlyen

Following are some of my own thoughts:

"Grief took more energy than I ever thought it would.

Hospice not only cared for us while my mom was dying, but they cared by visiting, calling and sending us a number of hand-outs concerning grief, hospice shock and coping for a year after Mom had died. God led me to share these with our church as a resource to others who are grieving.

Since my husband read all the hand-outs, he could see how I was doing and recognize any problems. He misses my mom too and has grieved for her as well. In spite of his own grief, he stepped in and prevented me from making some really stupid decisions on two occasions. I am so grateful for his love, strength, comfort and intervention. While grieving you can make some really irrational decisions that you may later regret. It is so true to not make any major decisions while you are grieving.

Thanks to my family and friends who continued to care by calling, sending cards, praying and asking how we were doing. I love you dearly. Life is precious and short. Tell the ones you love that you do love them. Someday you may not have the opportunity.

About a year and a half ago, I had prayed to God that I wanted to go deeper with Him. I have gone so much deeper in ways I did not expect, but would not change not only with my Lord, but also with my family. God is my Refuge, my Strength.

I will close with a Psalm very close to my heart: Psalm 63. May you desire to go deeper with God."

Kay

Psalm 63:1-8

"O God, you are my God,
earnestly I seek you;
my soul thirsts for you,
my body longs for you,
in a dry and weary land
where there is no water.

I have seen you in the sanctuary
and beheld your power and your glory.
Because your love is better than life,
my lips will glorify you.
I will praise you as long as I live,

and in your name I will lift up my hands.
My soul will be satisfied as with the richest of foods;
with singing lips my mouth will praise you.

On my bed I remember you;
I think of you through the watches of the night.
Because you are my help,
I sing in the shadow of your wings.
My soul clings to you;
your right hand upholds me."

Afterward

Strength for the Journey. God was my strength for this journey. He rained down and flooded my mind with Scripture after Scripture. All day. Every day. All those years that I had dug into His Word, meditated on it and took it to heart, God poured His Word back into me when I needed it most.

When you study the Bible, you store up those deposits. When the trials hit, and you haven't the energy to open the Bible, God floods your mind with His Word, His strength and His peace. He is my strength for this journey of life. Every day.

Strength for the Journey came also through the body of believers, whether they were friends or family. God provided them to minister to me through prayer, encouraging words through cards, phone calls, emails, the Caring Bridge® site, or face-to-face, through help with meals or gift cards for meals, through "Mom sitting", from driving the kids to emptying the apartment or sending a scrapbook for the pictures. God knew my needs and provided abundantly. He knows them now and still provides more than I ask or even imagine. He puts people in my life for strength for this journey.

God provided a wonderful hospice team from St. Cloud Hospital that helped give me strength for this journey, too. Each step of the way, they walked us through what to do to not only care for Mom, but to also make sure that as the primary care-giver, I was getting rest and relief too. They continued to care for me after Mom's death by visiting, calling and sending helpful information on grief and hospice shock as well as sending encouraging cards through the following year. All praise and glory to God, for He is Jehovah-Jireh!

Do you want to dig deeper into God's Word so you have strength for the journey? The following have helped me in digging deeper into God's Word: my husband who introduced me to BSF—Bible Study Fellowship[8], my friend, Karol-Rae, who introduced me to studying precept upon precept with Precept Ministries[9], my friend, Dawn Bengtson, who is as passionate about women knowing and digging into God's Word as I am and presented the Dig Deeper sessions with me, and my friends, family and Bible teachers who have encouraged and studied along with me. I am so grateful for the body of believers. May you find strength for the journey through Christ, His Word, and His Church. To Him be the glory! Forever! Amen.

About Kay

Kay Lukkarila is an author, Bible study leader, Sunday school teacher, wife, and mother of four who lives in Central Minnesota. She has a bachelor's degree in communication and has a passion for leading women in the study of God's word. Kay has been trained in inductive Bible study by Precept Ministries and has been trained in Bible Study Fellowship (BSF) as a group leader, children's leader and a substitute teaching leader.

Notes:

(1) Sona Mehring, *CaringBridge.Org.*
www.caringbridge.org/

(2) Lucado, Max. (2006) *Traveling Light.* Nashville, TN:
Thomas Nelson

(3) Bart Millard. "I Can Only Imagine" *The Worship Project* 1999

(4) Brenton Brown & Ken Riley. "Everlasting God"
Everlasting God, February 17, 2006

(5) Matt Redman. "Blessed Be Your Name" *Where Angels Fear to Tread,* 2002

(6) Todd Wuollet. "Soft and Tender Goodbye" June 6, 2008
www.youtube.com/watch?v=Cjo8vwLpjD8.

(7) Schweibert, Pat and DeKlyen, Chuck. (2005) *Tear Soup.*
5th edition, Portland, OR: Grief Watch

(8) *Bible Study Fellowship,* www.bsfinternational.org/

(9) *Precept Ministries,* www.precept.org/